TITANIA'S
NUMBER

TITANIA'S
NUMBER

3

Titania Hardie

CONNECTIONS
BOOK PUBLISHING

For Philip, Lawrence and S T Coleridge

A CONNECTIONS EDITION
This edition published in Great Britain in 2007 by
Connections Book Publishing Limited
St Chad's House, 148 King's Cross Road, London WC1X 9DH
www.connections-publishing.com

British Library Cataloguing-in-Publication data available on request.

ISBN 978-1-85906-225-8

1 3 5 7 9 10 8 6 4 2

Phototypeset in Bliss and Natural Script using QuarkXPress on Apple Macintosh
Printed in China

Contents

STARTING THE JOURNEY

This little book of numerology invites you to be amazed by what you will learn from numbers – about your character, your tastes, your instincts, your relationships, and even about your future. But to do this involves a willingness to believe – as Pythagoras, the 'Father of Numbers' did – that numbers can provide a clue, or formula, through which we can perceive some of the evolving patterns and cycles that affect our own individual existence.
Let's find out more ...

Discovering numerology

Fans of Sudoku will understand how it entices us intellectually to see how strands of numbers – almost magically – slot together and interconnect with one another, revealing a rhythm of harmonious relationships between the lines. In one sense, numerology does this for us on a personal and spiritual level. The Science of Numbers, as it is called, suggests that there is an order and a rhythm in the universe of which we are a part, and although there is a certain mystery in the way numbers seem to function as symbols for our experiences, there is a long tradition across many cultures of their fascination for us.

Now, in an age of gigabytes, PINs and mathematic-based technology, how can we doubt the role that numbers play, or the way in which they have become part of our daily landscape? Numbers speak to us every day about

2   1   9   8   7   6   5   4   3

our personal identity on this planet. Our birth date is absorbed by society as proof of our existence: you need it to be 'real' at the bank, in the office, when you travel, in an automated phone queue – in *all* official records. Indeed, many people consider the day-date of their birthday to be their lucky number. But can it really say anything about us?

Did you know, for instance, that:

- If you were a **5** or a **9**, you'd need to invest in good-quality luggage because you'd be bound to notch up a lot of air miles?
- Or that a **6** feels compelled to generously host open-house for guests and family?
- A **7** will want to specialize in whatever interests them?
- And an **8** would rather have one small quality gift than half a dozen less luxurious presents?
- Or that any friend who's a **4** will painstakingly spend

3　　4　　5　　6　　7　　8　　9　　1　　2

hours getting something just right, whereas a **1** will rush in and get several projects started, full of enthusiasm, only to leave someone else to carry them through to completion?

But you've picked *this* little volume because you're a **3**, which is the number of the entertainer who has so many gifts! You bring joy to others, and share your time with many people ... whereas, had you been a **2**, you would prefer to live quietly, with just one or two partnerships, both socially and in business.

About this book

Each individual title in this series investigates, in depth, the meaning of one of nine personal numbers. *This* volume is dedicated to the exploration of the number **3**.

We will be focusing principally on your **DAY** number –

2   1   9   8   7   6   5   4   3

that is, the number relating to the day of the month on which you were born (in your case, the 3rd, 12th, 21st or 30th of the month). Calculating your **DAY** number is easy: you simply add the digits of your day together (where applicable), and keep adding them until they reduce to a single number (*see calculation examples on page 270*). And that's it. It doesn't matter which month or year you were born in – you just need the day-date to discover your **DAY** number. And *you're* a **3**.

Your **DAY** number reveals all kinds of information, and, working from this number, we will be considering:

- The obvious attributes of your number as they impact on your personality
- How you are likely to dress, and what colours or styles appeal
- How you react to things psychologically, and what drives or motivates you

3   4   5   6   7   8   9   1   2

- In which fields you will have the most natural abilities and gifts
- What annoys you most
- What sort of lover you are, and how you relate to all other numbers
- What the future holds

... and much, much more.

And you have another significant number too: your **LIFE** number. This is derived from adding up the digits in the *whole* of your birth date – day, month and year (*see examples on page 270*). What does *this* number mean, and what do your **DAY** and **LIFE** numbers mean in tandem? And how does it affect you if you're also a 'master' number (**11** or **22**)? Read on and you'll see. But first, let's meet your **DAY** number ...

2   1   9   8   7   6   5   4   3

So, you're a 3

3

Imaginative **optimist** and warm-hearted friend, you are a **vibrant** person with an almost over-generous supply of talents and abilities – making it difficult, sometimes, to decide where to place your energies. You have a **highly creative** mind and love to dip into so many artistic areas, appreciating art and fashion, good food, beautiful buildings and picturesque vistas. You always have an **uplifting** effect on friends and family, with the capacity to jolt those who have lost their way, or become bogged down, out of their misery. You feel for others but in a **pragmatic** way, keeping your sense of humour in a crisis and showing them how to do so as well.

Naturally drawn to theatre and drama, you are gifted as both **actor** and mimic, but you can sometimes make a

3   4   5   6   7   8   9   1   2

drama out of your own life just to give you something to think about! Your powers of expression are convincing, and you love to **make people laugh** by showing them the absurd side of anything that is bringing them down — and you can even do this for yourself. You **communicate** particularly well, and it is usually in areas of communicative work that you will find your truest vocation. **3**s are born counsellors and therapists, blessed with the gift of the gab and a bubbly way of getting others to talk about themselves. Also, in your daily life you must breathe in **variety**, for a repetitive, banal job will undercut your strength — which is **flexibility**.

As the arts have such a pull on the creative mind of your number, you may feel frustration if you don't express your **artistic talent** in some sphere of your life. You also have a good ear for **language**: delving into several is in your interest, and will be easy to do — even if you never master one in its entirety. It is in your nature to sample and **enjoy**

numerous things on offer in life, and the lack of directive to specialize – which a **7** would need to do – is not something which really concerns you, or holds you back.

But this can sometimes bring a negative response too. You may be guilty of **scattering your energies** in too many directions, finding it impossible to make the most of your true talents. Or, just as frustratingly, your ability may not be endorsed by your circumstances, so that personal or work issues force you to **stretch yourself too thinly**; you may want to concentrate your time to a fruitful outcome, but can't. This may make you feel that you are forever postponing the achievement of something more important – which you know you could do, given a chance.

Nevertheless, optimism is inherent in your make-up, and you usually return to a **sunshine countenance** before the gremlins get you down. You radiate this sunshine to others too, and will be a **valued friend** to people who are dear to you in all kinds of places, with different backgrounds, or disparate values. You find something to appreciate in them all. And you are, for your part, **affable**, charming and **witty**, and those who meet you once don't want to lose you. You have style, and **bring pleasure** to those around you. Yet for all this — and despite having so many unusual friends — you are **loyal** beyond measure most of the time.

To make a success of your life, you will need to try to select what is most important to you. The **flair** you have in so many areas can pull you one way and then another, leaving you feeling you have wasted your time and ideas on unworthy people or ends. You may also have to guard against **financial extravagance** or recklessness, as any beautiful object that catches your eye can be the must-have object of the moment, though it has no lasting value.

You love **beauty** and beautiful people, and both find a natural place in your life. You also love to create **luxury** and pleasure for those you love, and may frequently go out of your way to find just the right gift or greeting. Half an hour with you has the impact of a '**rescue**' for so many people – even in business. But this should not suggest your mind is not **sharp**: you have a talent for writing, the use of words, and **seeing into the heart** of things. You are **inspirational** and **joy-giving**, and your life may be very full, and lead you along many unusual paths, for you to see yourself in all your colours!

Sound familiar? Getting a taste for what your number is about? And this is just the beginning. You'll soon find out how the number 3 expresses itself as your Day number in each and every day of your life. But before we go any further, let's take a look at where all this first came from ...

3   4   5   6   7   8   9   1   2

What's in a number?

Numbers have always had a sacred meaning. The Egyptians used an alphabet that conflated letters and numbers, and, as such, each number exuded an idea that was more than the sum it stood for. There is a whole book of the Old Testament devoted to the subject; and the Hebrew language – exactly like the Egyptian – has a magical subtext of meaning where letters and numbers can be doubled to reveal an extra layer of secret, so-called 'occult' information. It is called the *gematria*, and forms a crucial part of the sacred occult wisdom called Kabbalah. There were twenty-two letters – a master number – in both the Greek (Phoenician) and Hebrew alphabets, and repetitions of the spiritual properties of the numbers **3** and, especially, **7** recur throughout the Bible.

2 1 9 8 7 6 5 4 3

The Father of Numbers

But modern numerology derives more formally from Pythagoras, the Father of Numbers, who was a serious and spiritual philosopher, as well as the man who explained some of the secrets of geometry. Born on the island of Samos, although he ultimately settled in Cretona, a Greek colony in southern Italy, he is understood to have travelled widely to both Egypt and Judea. Some accounts of his life also suggest he may have studied under the Persian sages of Zoroaster, but an analysis of his teachings certainly reveals the strong influence of Kabbalistic thought in his philosophy.

Pythagoras understood numbers as a *quality* of being, as well as a *quantity* of material value. In one sense, the numbers as figures were connected with the measuring of things, but 'number' itself was significantly different to this, and encompassed a spiritual value. The numbers from one through to nine represented universal principles through which everything evolves, symbolizing even the stages an idea passes through before it becomes a reality. Mathematics was the tool through which we could apprehend the Creation, the universe, and ourselves. Musical harmony was a sacred part of this knowledge, as was geometry, which revealed divine proportion.

Most importantly, Pythagoras believed that numbers were expressive of the principles of all real existence – that numbers themselves embodied the principles of our dawning awareness, our conjecture and growth. Through mathematics and number we could approach divine wisdom and the workings of the universe as a macrocosm. Thus, in microcosm, our personal 'mathematics' would unlock the workings of our own being, and help us to see a divine wisdom concerning ourselves. **1** was not just the first digit, but also had a character of beginning, of independence, of leadership, just as the number **2** was more than merely the second number quantifying two objects, but also implied the philosophical concept of a pair, of co-operation, of a relationship beyond the individual.

Pythagoras also believed that we could understand our direction and fate through an awareness of repeating cycles of number, making numerology a key to revealing our opportunities and our destiny.

By tradition, the doctrine Pythagoras taught to his students in the sixth century BCE was secret, and no one wrote down his ideas until his death. But Plato was a follower of Pythagoras and, along with the rebirth of Platonism, the ideas of the Father of Mathematics were revealed afresh during the revival of Greek learning in the Renaissance. The great magi of the fifteenth and sixteenth centuries explored anew the significance of number and the gematria, to understand the hidden messages of the ancients and of the divine mind. Mathematics as a philosophy was the bridge to higher realms of spirituality.

Essence of the numbers

one is the spark, the beginning, Alpha, the Ego of
consciousness. It is male.

two is consort. Adding partnership, receptivity, it is female,
bringing tact.

three is a synthesizing of both of these qualities and brings
expansion and joy.

four is the number of the Earth, of the garden, and of
stability. It brings order.

five is curiosity and experiment, freedom, changes. It brings
sensuality.

six nurtures and cares for others. It will love and beautify,
and brings counsel.

seven perfects and contemplates the Creation. It is
intellect, stillness, spirit.

eight is the number of power, the octave, a higher
incarnation. It brings judgement.

nine is humanity, selflessness, often impersonal and all-
knowing. It brings compassion.

2   1   9   8   7   6   5   4   3

Applying the knowledge

A deeper understanding of the self can be achieved through an awareness of the mysticism of number within us; and both the birth date and, to some degree, our given name are the keys to unlocking our mystical, spiritual core of being. Exploring the affinity between letter and number can also reveal insights about the lessons we need to learn throughout our lives to improve and develop as individuals (*see page 25*).

This book looks at the significance of numbers as they affect us every day, focusing largely, as introduced earlier, on our **DAY** number. It is this number that reveals to us our instincts, our impulses, our natural tastes and undiluted responses, our talents and immediate inclinations. This is how people see us in daily situations, and how we behave by essence.

We will be exploring how our **DAY** number influences

our love relationships and friendships; at what it says about our career strengths and our childhood; at the way our number manifests in our leisure time; and at how it might give us a better understanding of what to expect in our future cycles, as we pass through any given year under the sway of a particular number. Each birthday initiates a new cycle, and each cycle seems uncannily connected with the philosophical concerns of the number which governs that year. Look both to the past and present to see how strongly the number-cycle can illuminate our experiences ... and then count ahead to ponder what may be in store over the next year or two.

And numbers also say something about where we live or work, about our car, and even about our pets. Understanding these secret qualities can add a new dimension of pleasure – not to mention surprise – to our journey through life.

A NUMBER TO GROW INTO

The presence of our **LIFE** number, however, takes longer for us to appreciate in ourselves — longer for us to grow into — and it often takes time to reveal itself. This number comes to the fore as your life progresses, and on pages 214–247 we will be looking at the meaning of your **DAY** number together with your individual **LIFE** number, to see what this reveals about your character and potentiality.

The **LIFE** number may intensify the experience of the **DAY** number — if it is closely related to it, or shares similar patterns. But more frequently our two different numbers clash a little, and this often allows insight into the aspects of our being where instinct pulls us in one direction but higher wisdom or experience mediates and pulls us in a second direction.

Who would have thought you could learn so much from a number? Pythagoras certainly did, over 2,500 years ago ... and now you will discover it too.

What's in a name?

Your name also has a story to tell, and it is a story revealed through number. Every letter corresponds to a number: in the Western alphabet we use twenty-six letters, which are at variance with the twenty-two formerly enshrined in the Hebrew and Greek alphabets. Some numerologists believe that this is in keeping with the more material world we now live in, as the number '26' reduces to '8' (when you add the digits), which is the number of power and money.

The correspondences between the numbers and the letters of the alphabet are as follows:

1	2	3	4	5	6	7	8	9
A	B	C	D	E	F	G	H	I
J	K	L	M	N	O	P	Q	R
S	T	U	V	W	X	Y	Z	

2	1	9	8	7	6	5	4	3

As you are a **3**, it is most revealing to look at the letters C, L and U as they occur (or not!) in your name. This is because they intensify the experience and impression of your main number.

To make the most of the qualities inherent in your number, you should be using a name which is in poetic harmony with your **DAY** number. As a **3**, you will radiate your powers of speech, wit and energy at their highest level of expression – helping you in your daily life – if you have a name which underlines these **3** qualities. Using a name which includes a C, L or U bolsters your powers. If this sounds strange, consider that many of us have our names shortened or played upon by friends, family and lovers, so it is important to feel that our chosen name – the one that we use as we go about in the world – is making the best of our abilities and energies.

Among the letters that are equivalent to the number **3**, L is a common consonant – so the chances are that you have an L in your name. It is especially significant if your name starts with one of these letters, for it introduces the strength of you number **3** right at the beginning of your name. Create a nickname with these letters in, if necessary, just to back up the outstanding properties of creativity that come with your number.

The letter-numbers help us to act out our sense of purpose, and if these work in correspondence with the DAY number we are more likely to find our sense of will and achieve our goals more rapidly. But if we have few, or none, of the letters of our DAY number, we often feel it is much harder to shine in our field of opportunity.

Missing a '3' letter?

As a **3**, you rely on expressing yourself with flair and confidence, but without a '**3**' letter in your name you will need to work on finding the best way to be heard. You may

2   1   9   8   7   6   5   4   3

also find that your natural sense of optimism is constantly challenged, if you are lacking an active '3' letter.

Those without any of these letters are likely to find it difficult to socialize or mix with new people, and this is crucial if you are a **3**. Find a way to include a C, L or U in your name, to override the lack. This will also be important in relation to your physical appearance, which is so important to your sense of identity: without a '**3**' letter you will struggle to feel confident about the way the world sees you. It's vital that you boost your sense of self in any way you can to offset this, as you feel (possibly rightly) that people are judging you by the way you present yourself. If you are choosing a business name, bear this in mind.

Too many 'C's or 'L's?

It can be just as much of a problem if your name carries a flood of letters which correspond to your number. This potentially gives you an overdose, and brings out some of the more negative qualities associated with **3**.

Too many '**3**' letters results in an intense energy and indecisiveness. If you have three or more 'C's or three or more 'L's, you may be too much of a chatterer, a person who cannot be still at all, and who feels the compulsion to give too much information to others out of nervousness. You may also suffer from throat infections or vocal weaknesses when you most need to speak! Several 'L's, especially, causes a physical freneticism that may make you trip over or drop things. Limit the number you use professionally, or in a romance, if you want to feel more focused and calm.

YOUR DAY NUMBER
It's a new day ...

You will learn a lot about the numbers of your birthday and your name as this book unfolds, but the DAY number is, to my mind, the most important – and sometimes least well-recognized – number of all ... the number which exerts a magnetic hold on us each and every day of our lives. Every time we react to a situation, an emotion, a provocation of any kind, we are shooting straight from the hip, as it were, and this reaction is coloured by our DAY number.

3   4   5   6   7   8   9   1   2

As we know, your 'Day Force', or **DAY**, number is **3** if you were born on the 3rd, 12th, 21st or 30th of any month. Each of these different dates also affects us – the characteristics of the number derived from a birthday on the 12th vary intriguingly from one on the 30th, for instance – and we will look at these differences in the pages ahead.

All four dates, however, still reconcile to an overall **3**. This number determines your gut reactions and the way you express yourself when you are being most true to yourself. Your parents, lovers, friends and co-workers all know you best through this number.

So what is the theme of being a 3? What are you like when you're at work, rest and play? And how compatible are you with the other numbers? Let's find out …

2 1 9 8 7 6 5 4 3

3'S CHARACTER
Charms, graces, warts and all ...

Lit by an internal eye that sees delight in the world – and always expecting unlimited potential for personal happiness – 3 is one of nature's charmers. Born with this number influencing you every day, you have an excellent eye for colour, an ear for music and a true appreciation of beauty and aesthetics. You are talkative, playful, good-humoured and a born communicator, and you love to chat in a friendly way with anybody, making friends easily wherever you go.

Your communication skills affect your capacity to write, speak, sing – which you may do often – and act. Many **3**s choose to be actors – or may be frustrated thespians – for this number is unquestionably born to bask in the limelight, one way or another, and you are talented in many directions artistically.

On the ball

This is a **DAY** number which blesses you with sharp mental skills and a quick rejoinder in conversation. Your alert brain loves to acquire new information: a juggler keeping several balls in the air at a time is a good emblem for **3**s, as your hands can be quite busy but yet you can still toss another subject up into the air and keep everyone entertained. You are usually interested – and gifted – in more subjects than one, rather like your corresponding astrological sign, Gemini, which is just such another delightful chatterbox!

2   1   9   8   7   6   5   4   3

All manner of entertainment brings out the best in you, especially when you are playing host to a crowd from work, or a gaggle of perfect strangers who have just arrived from out of town. You manage to give even the coffee break a party feel, and get your cohorts laughing and relaxing in seconds. And you come to life at any serious party ...

Host with the most

If you're the host you will have chosen everything with care to a themed agenda, paying attention to colour and the ambience of the décor, just as much as what's on the menu and which kindred souls should be there. Your optimum wish is that everyone will leave feeling elated, their minds buzzing, so you choose friends and the appropriate feast to arrive at that end. Your personal contribution outstrips even the delicious food, so that you assume the role of Master of Ceremonies, ordering and hailing a sequence of sensual delights that will bring out the childish wonder in your guests — however hardened they are to life. You also feel perfectly at home keeping the conversation bubbling along, ensuring that every guest feels special, and is spoken to — and heard. No number (not even gracious **6**) is a better host to such a diverse cast of friends and acquaintances.

Despite being a party animal, you are likely to have only a few *really* good friends, but these are of both sexes, all races and every persuasion. They are all equally drawn to your lovely gentle humour, your amazing general knowledge and your unforced charm. Somehow, you have a subject to share with everyone — even your partner's recluse cousin from the far north, or the man who empties your garbage! — finding common ground, in fact, on a regular basis with the most unlikely companions. There may be some confused people around you who would say you have no discrimination when it comes to your friends, but this is unfair. You are simply tolerant where others may not be!

Keynotes of the 3 personality

Positive associations: imaginative power, visual creativity, childlike quality, prone to occurrence of fairy-tale events, 'laughing' character, positive outlook, sanguine emotions, vivid personality, good host and friend

Negative associations: financially extravagant, chatterbox to no effect, aimless, indecisive, inability to put weight behind projects, moody, sometimes selfish, childish, irrational, plays the field emotionally

Express yourself

One of your primary concerns in life is self-expression. Apart from the obvious way in which this manifests – with your jokey sense of humour and perfect choice of word for every occasion – you will want, and need, to beautify your surroundings ... and seeing the results of your efforts will satisfy you. Your artistic eye is very sound and, though you will not necessarily opt for anything too avant-garde, you do show originality and flair within the limits of what others would still regard 'good taste'. It *must* have originality, though – for, if someone else has done it, you will want to stamp on your own sense of self.

You are sometimes very proud, and yet **3**s can also be proud of humble beginnings too. You may feel a kind of reverse dignity in having come from nothing to become more comfortable and an achiever – and you will enjoy being able to show generosity to your family and siblings if this happens. But you are also very ambitious, impulsive and *intolerant* – particularly if anyone crosses you. You need plenty of scope in any job or domestic situation to allow you to develop your quirky sense of humour, as this is one of your best attributes, bestowed upon you to divert and inspire others. This sense of humour also helps you to learn, as you mature, to nullify your propensity to nervousness and a possible lack of direction. Gradually you will understand how to keep your wandering mind and high level of energy tied down in one place just long enough to achieve your inspired goals.

The road to happiness

You must try to avoid an inherent pull to be just a clever dilettante, and hone one or two of your brightest talents until you can see a tangible outcome from them. If your work is *too* routine, though, you will soon lose interest and want to find an outlet for your creativity. Personal freedom is quite essential to your happiness, at home and at work, and you will prefer doing almost anything as long as it's not strictly nine-to-five. You must also curtail your tendencies to worry, and instead try to make the best of any situation, seeing the funny side of it and amusing others while you're about it. At certain intervals in your life you

3 4 5 6 7 8 9 1 2

will recognize moments when — all on your own — you are behaving like a pair of clowns: both happy and sad, your vacillating moods may change from miserable to euphoric in a matter of moments. But all will be well if you remember that you *are* a clown — and revel in that — so that your humour becomes your best restorative. You will always feel justified in all your pain and drama when you have converted a room full of forlorn faces to ones of merriment.

In the money

Most people with **3** birthdays are lucky with money, though you will have to hold on to this when the roller-coaster inevitably takes you down for a spell or two. Fortunately, you can be creative, and have the knack of inspiration at your fingertips when you have to find a way out of temporary financial trouble. Work connected with the media, or in the public eye, will usually be your best

2   1   9   8   7   6   5   4   3

chance of finding happiness and fulfilment, but you are also well suited to a career in public relations and publicity, or organizing professional parties and functions. You have gifts in designing, decorating and writing too, as well as in spa therapies and beauty work. And you are, of course, an excellent teacher or lecturer – especially of young children – and your work will always demand that you be a talker and an actor in some way, whatever the field.

Young at heart

To make the best use of your energy and popularity, and to keep you lucky with money and friends, remember to use a name with the letters C, L or U somewhere in it. The letter L, especially, helps you to feel optimistic, and brings out your bouncing agelessness. **3**s do have a lovely child-like aspect to their character, never growing old them-selves, always able to bring fresh enthusiasm to the little surprises in life. This also means that, as a **3**, you communicate with children as though you were one of them, and you know just how to win their hearts.

It's from this aspect of your character, however, that your greatest weakness also arises: your childlike inclination to rush into too many things, your ability to turn your hand to various tasks. You run the risk of being the dilettante rather than the specialist, and of dividing your energies into too many outlets, never achieving a sufficient degree of focus on any one of them! Try to balance your energies more, finish the wonderful, imaginative things you start, and avoid the frustrations you run into when you over-extend yourself.

To be sure of being happy in your heart, find a soulmate who is flexible and humorous too — someone who will recognize your mood swings and not take them personally. We shall have much more to say about your love life a little later on, but it is interesting to note that a **3** may be better off with another **3** emotionally than with almost any other number. This is not universally true: most numbers need some change of direction in their partner. **3**, however, shines in the company of another **3** – and the two numbers added together make **6**, which is the number of love. Perhaps only another **3** understands why so many clever ideas remain unrealized, or why you have such a number of unfinished tasks around you. One of your worst failings, as a **3**, is the problem of scattering your energies to no effect.

Feed your mind

If you find no proper expression for your acuity, you may become critical – even gossipy – of others, or say clever but hurtful things just for entertaining effect. The only sound remedy for this is to give your mind a problematic bone to chew over – to educate and expand your awareness beyond your situation. **3**s make excellent students, and want to learn, so this should be a priority as you go through life. You also, quite simply, need to keep busy!

3s also have an exceptional imaginative power – and this may be one of the talents that most affects your life. You can enter into something completely – a book, a film, the past – and your mind can range across time and space with visions of what is possible, and what you wish to become. And, with your power to see things vividly, you may very well make them happen. This is what is meant by having the power to literally make your wishes become real.

More than meets the eye

You will confound every person who thinks they 'know' you, for there is always more to discover about a **3**. You may feel spiritual, and recognize inner words of truth; or you may be a cynic who is unconvinced by what you hear concerning faith. Perhaps you're someone who needs to surround themselves with luxury and extravagance, or maybe you're happy simply with two or three friends and a bottle of table wine on a beach. You can adapt to most situations very well, and your willingness to play along – to try any number of things at least once – earmarks you. You are never completely practical, but other numbers willingly come to your rescue and help to enact the imaginative thoughts that come from you. And you are never, ever alone.

3 in a nutshell

Personality watchwords: pleasure-loving, laughter-inducing, raconteur

Lucky colours: rose, ruby

Lucky herbs/flowers: snapdragon, iris, parsley

Scents: tea rose, bergamot, lime

Fashion style: colourful, expensive, in vogue

Decorative style: arty, thematic, preference for 1920s/1930s taste?

Letters: C, L or U (needed in the name you use)

Car style: roof down, all-weather fun vehicle – any colour except black

Holiday destination: anywhere!

Which 3 are you?

8 9 1 2 **3** 4 5 6 7

Everyone with a **DAY** number of **3** will exhibit many of the characteristics just discussed. It is interesting to see, though, how the number **3** varies across all of its incarnations. There is a subtle but definite difference between the way the number operates for someone born on the 3rd of the month – which makes for a pure **3** effect – and someone born, say, on the 21st.

As a rule, anyone born on the single-digit date has the truest and most undiluted effect from the number, whereas someone born as a product of two digits borrows some qualities from the pairing of the numbers. Twenty-anything puts the softening digit '2' before the second number, and this usually means that, whatever number you are, you are more aware of the needs of others. Similarly, if '1' is the first digit (12th), you are more independent, and perhaps more assured of your self-worth, than other people. The '3' in '30th' adds an extra dimension to the power of the **3** itself: you have ten times the amount of **3** charisma and charm!

Let's look at the variations across all the birthdays . . .

2   1   9   8   7   6   5   4   3

Born on the 3rd?

With the purest form of this **DAY** number as your birthday,
your ability as a writer should be particularly pronounced.
You are especially energetic when inspired by anything –
and this helps you recover from sadness or illness fairly
quickly. Even when there is a mountain of hard, physical
work to get through, you can tirelessly propel yourself to
the very last stages before you stop and actually realize
the magnitude of what you've taken on. You may discuss
plans fully before you begin any task, but once you do
decide on the best way forward, you like to get on with
things – especially once they've been agreed with a third
party. You seem compliant in all of these undertakings, but
you can be surprisingly bossy and even stubborn if anyone
tries to interfere once your mind is made up.

   Your imagination is very vivid, even to the point where

3   4   5   6   7   8   9   1   2

you may dwell slightly in a fantasy land. You have good storytelling powers, though, and you relate straightforward tales in a highly amusing anecdotal fashion, enabling you to spin simple yarns into money-earning short stories if you want to, or to talk entertainingly at public functions. All **3** birthdays have the gift of the proverbial gab, but there is no better person to be a best man or the compere at a social function.

And you love showbiz – from very popular shows and films to more challenging cultural forms. You have a witty way of interpreting plays and poetry verbally, with a talent for review, and for expressing pithy criticisms with gusto. You may also love to read – anything from short stories to demanding trilogies – and you may dabble in several different languages without ever feeling the need to perfect any. At least you can have brief and meaningful conversations with a cast of thousands, and you are a very expressive person.

2   1   9   8   7   6   5   4   3

Finding the perfect career could be difficult, because you are truly spoiled for choice, yet it's likely you can't – or won't – settle on what you really enjoy for some time. Travel may be quite important to you, so you could feel pulled in this direction work-wise; or, at least, you will be happier if you can move around freely during the course of a day, rather than being stuck behind a desk or in a sedentary position. Travel allows you to become interested in a variety of experiences, encourages you to sample fresh opportunities constantly. You certainly need to work with people, speaking to them and enticing them to talk to you. You are a great counsellor, teacher, lecturer, public relations consultant. For these reasons, you could choose to be a good lawyer, actor or writer; and any work centred on theatre, film or television would be a natural choice – especially as it affords you changeability.

Be careful not to stretch yourself too thinly across too many obligations: you have many talents, and could find you end up taking on more than is good for you. Try to perfect one thing as your main area of industry, and specialize in this. Over-indulgence and extravagance are also possible pitfalls, as you never know when it is 'enough'. But you should be lucky in what comes to you in life, and have a nose for a good speculative venture. Even your circle of friends may bring good fortune – for you are certainly going to meet lots of people who can make things happen.

Born on the 12th?

If your **3 DAY** number derives from a birthday on the 12th, you have an exceptional tolerance for a multiplicity of beliefs and ideas. You are vibrantly artistic and have a wonderful eye for all things visual (thus career options, for you, include many types of design). You may even have a complex understanding of what is illusion and what is reality, and your ideas are a cut above the common way of seeing things. You have poise and dignity, though you can be quite mad if the mood takes you somewhere playful.

Gifted at writing, like a pure **3**, and having a sense of the right phrase or slogan that will work well in advertising, you may decide journalism or copywriting is your thing. You also have considerable skill with colour, line and image, and your flair for the dramatic is highly developed. If coupled with **3**'s usual dramatic interest, film will be your special medium, and, whether you work in this indus-try or another field which makes use of similar talents, you will probably love to chill out in a crisis by spending a day watching old movies.

Knowing when people dear to you are in trouble or suffering, you come to the rescue with material and verbal offerings. Perhaps you bring flowers, post a card or send an e-mail, just to make a hug happen in a special, unusual way. The consummate party-thrower, you take great care in the presentation of gifts, in the preparation for projects, in the organization of venues for entertaining.

You have an interesting sense of what is karma, under-standing cause and effect in a special way, and have an innate sensitivity to the fact that afflictions are often caused by us – a result of our own conscious or uncon-scious choices. This makes you a wise friend who knows how to let go when – or if – the time comes. You're not afraid to go against the grain of what is considered right, or in good taste. Many times in your life you will suffer reversals of fortune, but you will probably respond to this by flipping your own sense of balance up the other way, and landing safely on your feet again.

On the positive side, peace and tranquillity come to you in many guises, and you can be extraordinarily philosophical in the way you handle people, relationships and work responsibilities. You see to the heart of what is troubling the world, and your work is an effort to redress this balance, ever so slightly. You will place great emphasis on the aesthetic, creating as much beauty around you as you can. You will also make some sacrifices, but they are largely voluntary, and, even when you feel compelled to make them, you'll look for the best in whatever results. No public opinion, no adverse circumstances, really disturb your inner being, and you have courage under considerable duress.

On the minus side, your '12' is a more nervous variation of **3**, and you must curb your impatience with others a little. You may have a dark side, and you could feel your friendships with others are largely superficial. Remaining passive is often the best way to ameliorate sour notes in relationships, and it will usually be better if you don't go after something, but let it come to you. Much in life is thrown at you to test your sense of acceptance, and when you show you can resist the temptation to let your clever tongue cut into others, you will achieve what you wanted from the beginning. Patience is an issue for you! Intellectual stimulation will help you absorb your nervous impulses, but if you have a strong number like **4** or **7** as your LIFE number (*see page 214*), you may be too analytical and take nothing as straightforward or simple. You need to take some things on trust.

2   1   9   8   7   6   5   4   3

Born on the 21st?

This birthday is generally one of very good fortune. You have talents and charms and luck, and a way of looking at the world which ensures you have friends and lovers who truly care for you. You should lead a life which brings you into contact with music and dance, as you have excellent rhythm.

You need lots of affection, but you sometimes suffer an emotional roller-coaster ride, turning hot and cold in your reactions to things and people. This, in turn, can lead to periods of depression (always short-lived) and moodiness, so in a relationship your lover must be a good friend as well – someone able to step back and leave you alone without undue worry if you're suddenly grumpy or withdrawn. These moods are just rain-showers on otherwise sunny days!

| 3 | 4 | 5 | 6 | 7 | 8 | 9 | 1 | 2 |

You enjoy reading as well as writing, and journalism often suits those with your birthday, as does work in education, writing, art or public relations. You love art, knowing what may make a good investment, and, as ever, you make friends with everyone you work alongside. In fact, working alone is actually not a good idea for you, because firing your ideas off others leads you to greater and greater creativity.

Though true of all **3**s, you, in particular, have an especially good memory, which blends with your positivism to make you lucky in life. It's likely that you never forget a name, or what someone was doing when last you spoke to them: and they appreciate the feeling of intimacy this creates. Or, in a business meeting, you are able to pick up exactly where you left off earlier, and maintain a sanguine outlook about where you are going in the future as a company – and the effect is to create a good impression all around you. This will always help you get on in the world.

And what is also especially true for someone with your particular birthday – and not always with other **3**s – is that you have patience, and this helps you to recognize limitations in a framework or situation, and to wait it out. These qualities give you, perhaps, the best chance of being a high achiever rather than just a gifted dreamer.

All **3** birthdays have a talent for the arts, but yours is notably literary, and a birthday on the 21st is the most likely to belong to a writer. Not only are you expressive, but you have wisdom and a concern for the world and the people in it, so you always find inspiration for what you want to say. With this comes a restlessness to live in various places and observe the conditions of the world, so you may be the best-travelled **3**, as well.

The negative connotations of this birthday might suggest you could become selfish or too inward-looking, if you find it hard to keep lasting friendships or relationships. Or, you may be stubborn and ignore the lessons

that you seem to be shown regularly. But your tru
is to show others the way, to inspire and amuse but a.
lift those around you to greater awareness. This is a gifted
number **3**.

Born on the 30th?

The added strength and vision from the zero in your birth date gives you considerable courage and drive in life. You are more concerned with achieving perfection, and leaving a lasting legacy, than any of the other **3**s. Whatever you choose in life – your career, your relationships, where you live, the path of study you select from the outset – are all choices made to ensure that you can do something worthwhile, and succeed.

At work you are very amusing and lively, but you need a great deal of free rein for your projects, and would be the unhappiest of all the **3** 'Day Force' variations if you were too strongly confined. Your self-expression and individuality are magnetic, but on a down day you are nervous, easily exhausted and indecisive. You may combat this with any number of meditative ploys, such as the use of calm-

ing colour and décor, soothing musical sounds in the b...
ground, or room fragrance, to gently recover your dignity
and think with serenity again. You are sometimes especially
stubborn in your ideas, and will benefit from listening to
the cheering advice of others.

Your number is well suited to a career that offers you
scope and responsibility – something that's not always one
of **3**'s strengths. You find it no difficulty to handle demanding projects or duties because you have a more organized
way of tackling tasks than **3**s usually do. With the typical
3 trait for talk and evaluation of people and circumstances,
this ability to deal with a broader spectrum in life would
make you an excellent barrister or high-court judge. You
are able to see the whole picture, and articulate what you
see with skill.

In addition, you perhaps may seem less eccentric
than some **3**s, which makes you a good ambassador when
you are dealing with more conventional kinds of people.

You argue for — and get — what you want, as you seem so safe and sane to others.

Drama and creative writing come as easily for you as for all the other 3s, though you are also quite interested in occult subjects. Your mind turns to higher matters, and you may have strongly spiritual feelings about the world, and recognize as superficial vanities all that is material and transitory. This said, you do still like to have aesthetically pleasing objects around you, and you will beautify your environment — and should have the money to do so; money comes rather easily for you, and you are generous to others too.

As well as the dramatic/theatrical possibilities open to you, you would enjoy any career path that involves music, teaching, or aspects of social work. Like all 3 DAY numbers, you attract a party atmosphere around you wherever you work — however serious the environment.

No doubt having a considerably magnetic personality

3   4   5   6   7   8   9   1   2

helps you through life: it is a special gift from the gods! But you have a philosophical side which adds weight and intellect to your lighter gifts of charm, and this is what makes you respected and beloved by such an array of people.

3 AT WORK

So, what kind of employee does your number make you? We've already seen that your birthday suggests you are much more comfortable working in a close partnership, but when you are in a large group, how do you fit in? If you're the boss, are you a good one? Which fields are likely to be the best for your talents? And which the worst? And what about the male/female divide? Is a 3 female boss more desirable than a 3 male colleague?

Here, we get to grips with your career potential, your needs and 'must-have's for job satisfaction, and your loves and loathes work-wise, hopefully highlighting some areas where there is room for you to adjust your manner around others, to help you achieve what it is you're aiming for.

3	4	5	6	7	8	9	1	2

In the marketplace

Your number might be deemed the 'I think' of numerology, rather like the first Air sign of the zodiac, Gemini. This means that, whether you are just starting out at work or are a seasoned professional, your mind is alert and always thinking of new things to do and ways to satisfy new curiosities.

You will keep a level of buoyant energy bubbling around you, and others will feel your enthusiasm and respond to it positively. And again, whether you are a junior or a company vice president, everyone will want to discuss ideas with you, or run suggestions past you for approval: you have what it takes to get toes tapping and minds whirring. Even when you rise to the top, you are still willing to listen to others, and to throw ideas around to get something just right.

2   1   9   8   7   6   5   4   3

VARIETY IS THE SPICE OF LIFE

Work will only ever attract and excite you if there is a changing weekly menu. If one job spills on too long, your boredom threshold sets in, for you need to move along quickly and see results early. This said, your imagination fires you to get on enthusiastically, and you will often carry the less inspired for the requisite miles to ensure a project or contract gets under way. You inject energy and pride in doing something a little differently – and you are almost always willing to tackle as many tasks as are necessary just to coax the less visually inclined to wade in and get their own hands dirty. Your keen mind is never above a little manipulation to get someone off their behind and into the job at hand!

Mediocrity is not something you will tolerate – either in people or in a job itself. You are quite idealistic about work, and would like to think that whatever you do will make a difference somewhere. In fact, you may be something of a crusader – especially if you are well educated and feel that you have the methods at your disposal to back up your ideas and suggestions career-wise. You long for a sense of justice, for people to behave as they should, and with warmth towards one another, and you often have the effect of spreading this bonhomie around you at work, which makes you popular and gains admiration in some surprising quarters. If there is little you can do to alter the nature of work you are involved in, you will certainly strive to alter the tone – from indifference to enthusiasm. Why should anyone spend their working hours being flat and uninvolved, you wonder? And you frequently carry your point, and add jollity to the atmosphere.

WHERE DOES YOUR LIGHT REALLY SHINE?
Here are some of the qualities that **3**s bring to any job:
- A poetic nature makes you a little romantic, and you dream of inspirational ways of moving the performances

of your work companions up a gear, so that everyone is at their peak – and you usually achieve this. This always brings you some responsibility and leadership.

- Your imagination works in tandem with a good intellect, and you look for more expansive and sophisticated ways of tackling any ventures. You can also be quite emotional when the occasion demands it, and this fuels your drive and lifts others along with you – making you a good team leader or motivator.

- You love things that are beautiful, and many possessions become valuable to you, so work that supports your own desire to collect such items and also, if possible, allows you to spend your work time in an aesthetic world offers an excellent area for expression work-wise, and provides a good channel for success.

- Despite a reputation for being giddy and excitable at times, you are surprisingly persistent and very dependable, as long as you believe in what you are doing –

which is crucial for your vocational happiness. High personal ideals mean you must also give your company or business the best work you are capable of. You will either work with gusto for your employer, or, if you're the boss, you will expect this same courtesy from your staff. This usually means that everything ticks along nicely.

- You will hardly be at your best if you are forced to work in a routine situation with little chance to show either your creativity or verbal skills. If you are absolutely compelled to be both practical and conservative, you must find a secondary outlet for your artistic energy — or think of a career change!

So, beauty, fellow-feeling, emotional contact with others, communication possibilities, and — above all — a variety of duties are all requisite elements in your work portfolio, if you are to live at your best. You want the nice things in life, and are willing to give a great deal to achieve them, so your work must be inspirational and have scope for you to flourish. But personal satisfaction and achievement only come if your work offers you a chance to be appreciated, and to work with something creative. Some of these careers may just fit the bill ...

Entertainment industry Your gift for words and mimicry makes you a natural performer, so whether you choose to work in front of an audience or to write scripts and plots for others, you may have a real gift in this field. Behind-the-scenes work as a director, photographer or agent for talent is also something that could attract you, and you are likely to be more than able to lend a hand – whether in amateur productions or as your full-time job – in lighting, designing, choreographing and illustrating. Thus theatre, publishing and music may all appeal as a career direction.

'Feel-good factor' careers A love of fantasy and the dream-world may entice you to work in some other aspect of literature or as a counsellor drawn to analysis. Your number is excellent at creating fantasy for others, which has an endless variety of expressions in the workplace – as a travel organizer or tour guide, as a professional party-planner, on committees which are involved in charitable work and fund-raising, or in the realm of relaxation and unwinding. If you open a bed-and-breakfast it will have the luxury feel of a small-scale Ritz – such is your attention to detail and your quest to provide that feel-good factor.

Real estate Real estate could be something of interest, mainly because of the potential to chat to clients, to move around during the day, and because your charm makes you a good salesperson. You also know what is appealing to others, and would be a good adviser for a vendor in the property market. **3**s often seem to make, at the very least, some additional income from an interest in property or speculation in the property market.

Luxury goods Luxury goods could be the basis of a business for you – either creating them, selling them, providing them or marketing them. Again, this has many possible manifestations – as, arguably, television, the restaurant trade, hospitality, the travel industry and luxury gifts all come under this banner. You definitely know what will excite someone's sensual appetite – and how to package this, as well.

Law/legal services Law, and drawing up contracts, suits the verbal fencing skills of a **3**, and a career in any work which demands such elements will enthral you. You love justice, and enjoy a good argument, so the legal field will always hold some fascination, and would make a good vocational direction.

Therapeutic work Therapy of any kind suits **3**'s people skills – which are almost second to none. You know how to make people open up and talk to you, and what's more you really care about how they are feeling, so in any area of work that involves therapy of any kind, you are going to shine. Marry this to your strangely prophetic skills – not so much reading people's inner thoughts as seeing a vision of where they are headed – and you would be a talented psychoanalyst, lifestyle coach or other kind of 'life' guide. Most people trust you and feel your sincerity – but you also have the humour to make them laugh, and rally them when they are being too self-indulgent. Many jobs require skills of therapy – whether they are strictly therapeutic or not! – and you may be a liaison or union representative, regardless of your 'official' work description.

Art critic, reviewer, columnist It goes without saying that **3**s have a witty way of summing up what is funny or touching in the world around us, and an excellent head for the arts generally. All kinds of writing and reviewing of this kind, therefore, suit a **3**'s varied skills.

Science and IT These fields will work for **3** if the job description itself revolves around people skills and a variety of talents. Being sequestered away, doing research or working alone, is more the domain of a **7** or a **1**, but **3** will enjoy any work that provides a mental challenge and then requires communicating to others.

This list isn't exhaustive – a **3** will find a way of bringing their own gifts to any job – but it does offer a good idea of the kinds of subject that should appeal to your number. Whatever the field, the need for talking with others and putting smiles on faces is at the root of **3**'s business talent.

And for luck?

Whatever your work, you will achieve your maximum potential if you use a name to work with that includes the letters C, L or U. Remember this when you are choosing a company name, if you go into partnership. It will help, too, for you to optimize your energy and positive attitude, if you decorate your work environment in the ruby-russet colours of a summer sunrise. If you are going for an important interview, these colours would make a positive choice in your outfit, as they help you to project yourself in your most attractive and sensitive light.

The 3 female boss

Tossing a silky scarf across her shoulder and **breezing** past the executives without apology for being late, the **3** woman in charge is a true wonder of the business world. A thousand things intervene when she is en route to the office, and she is **undaunted** by the myriad demands on her personal appearances: this is just how she likes it. No one holds it against her, for everyone knows she is something of a **butterfly**, resting in one place only long enough to bring colour and dash and movement to the stasis that existed before her arrival. She **varies her tone** from place to place – **childlike** with the newest recruits and full of **persuasive** feminine charm with her peers, yet able to sprinkle jaw-dropping one-liners liberally when she is in party mode out of hours. **3** is a miracle of light and

3   4   5   6   7   8   9   1   2

breeze. You fall under her spell, or you don't: there is no way to change her!

First command to new workers on the team will be **not to underestimate** their **3** female boss. She may appear youthful, even childlike, in her enthusiasm and humour, but she is **smart as a whip** and takes no nonsense from anyone. If she likes you she'll move heaven and earth to accommodate your needs and fears, but if she thinks you are slow-witted, or lacking enthusiasm for the task she has set you, she will find a withering remark which makes you feel as though you are in kindergarten.

The **3** female boss will **turn her hand** to any job a project requires, and look sassy and delighted about all of it – but she expects her juniors to do the same. Come to that, she expects her peer group to do the same. No one is above any job asked of them. But she does make it **fun** just to be on board!

2   1   9   8   7   6   5   4   3

WORK PROFILE
The 3 male boss

Seemingly easy-going and inclined to get along with just about everyone, don't mess with the **gentle manner** of the **3** male in his empire. He will always listen to reason, and if you have an excuse not to be somewhere he will be remarkably kind about it – but if you think he is a pushover as long as you ask with charm, don't be misled; he has written the rule book on this subject, and **knows when he is being conned**. A **3** male boss has so many facets to his nature he is always a **challenge to know well**. He will give you a longer lunch hour or let you work from home – just as long as the quality of your work is outstanding. He wants your enthusiasm and **commitment** and energy all day, every day, and if you show signs of flagging he will remember. And, strangely, you really want this man's

| 3 | 4 | 5 | 6 | 7 | 8 | 9 | 1 | 2 |

approval, because his **good opinion** and easy manner help the day go smoothly, and the sun shine brightly.

In fact, many people have a little crush on their **3 male boss** – because he is **different** without being scary. He has a good speaking voice and **dashing humour**, dresses well and knows when you are wearing designer clothes, notices a new fragrance when you are modelling one, and will tell you when your new haircut looks terrific. Or, if you lose his respect for any reason, he will say something pithy about that new haircut that makes you wish you'd kept it long. But when you need a pat on the back to finish an arduous task, or a kind word spoken because your mum is ill, somehow he knows, and **says exactly the right thing**.

Familiar by first name to everyone, the **3 male boss** is an **exemplary** manager of people's skills, and everyone goes out on a limb for him. But oh! – balancing that social calendar of his ... now *there's* a sleight-of-hand trick!

WORK PROFILE
The 3 female employee

Adding an **air** of something to the workplace, the **3** female employee arrives during her first week with a **familiarity** and **ease** that is the envy of her co-workers. She **smiles** and dresses distinctively, remembers everyone's names and brings cookies to put beside the kettle. And her mug is stylish, and tells you something about her you didn't know – a secret waiting to emerge, that she's an amateur actress, or has a beautiful singing voice. How does it tell you all that? It doesn't – but she does, while she's making you a cup at the same time. She can fit in such a lot of things on the hop, and **never miss a beat**.

If you weren't previously in the habit of telling anyone at work about your private life, the **3** working beside you changes all that. She has such a **charming** way of getting

| 3 | 4 | 5 | 6 | 7 | 8 | 9 | 1 | 2 |

you to talk, and knows just what to advise you about how to keep your lover interested, what to choose for your aunt's birthday, or how to brave your bank manager for a loan. Your **3** work friend is **fearless** and charming, and you will **learn a lot** if you listen to what she says about getting on in this world. And when life becomes too stressful, she'll buy you a drink and **make you laugh**, and you'll soon set everything to rights again.

But she can **drive you mad**, as well: too many ideas about things you may feel shouldn't concern her? Too much lip gloss? Too much of a flirt? But it is her natural way, and it will be better to **go with the flow** and enjoy the atmospheric change that occurs when she is there. She may seem flighty at times, or too interested in office gossip, but she is one **smart cookie** who knows more than you think about the way people act and what they want. If you want to enjoy your work more, team up with the **3** female employee. She's going places!

2   1   9   8   7   6   5   4   3

WORK PROFILE
The 3 male employee

He may not seem overtly ambitious, but the young male **3** starting a new job is going to **make a splash**. He sets a trend when he arrives – a style of dress, perhaps, or a new vocabulary that quickly catches on. He **wins his boss's confidence** with his willingness to learn everything in the first three or four days – which is really because he is as **enthusiastic** as a puppy, with no regrets that he is doing what he is doing.

He carries a **zest for life** with him, and he is so funny when he recounts his first day over a glass of something cold in the wine bar. He has such a **good demeanour** that – even if everyone may have been a little sceptical before he started – he wins a grudging **admiration** from the toughest cynic. He has a little bit of knowledge about a great many things, and his **jokey** way of getting through drudgery helps everyone endure a difficult day.

But what about that smile that seems permanently etched on his face: can that be real? Is he actually so good-natured and self-assured? It's a **boyishness** that is genuine, and the smile comes from the acute awareness that making a **pleasure** of work for others makes it more of a pleasure for him. He is **sincere**, but if you get on the wrong side of his acid wit you will set up a stint of verbal sparring that might be better avoided. As kind and resilient as the **3** man at work can be, he **can be cruel**, too, if he feels that he is being spoken down to, or not allowed to use his brain. He may not be vicious – as an irritated **7** might – but he doesn't like **criticism** at all, especially if it comes from someone he feels is his intellectual inferior. But he'll be very funny railing against it!

Ideal world or cruel world?
Best and worst jobs ...

IN AN IDEAL WORLD

Best job for a 3 female: Presenter of children's pop programme, or star in a sitcom about a law firm (plenty of scope for artistic talents and chance to offer comedic, swift rebukes to anyone who doesn't like the show)

Best job for a 3 male: Gentleman with a huge country manor, playing host to a variety of guests, and introducing artists to entrepreneurs (uses all **3**'s best skills and achieves a beautiful, aesthetic end product)

IN A CRUEL WORLD

Worst job for a 3 female: Working in a library (plenty of intellectual scope, but forced to be silent!)

Worst job for a 3 male: Growing produce on a small island (lovely space to think for one day, then a feeling of withdrawal from the vibrant world and no one to 'play with')

3'S CHILDHOOD

Seeing the way a number expresses itself in someone very young is fascinating, for the tendencies and responses are all in their infancy — and yet plain to see. Some facets of a number's power need to be grown into, and take time to reveal how they will be dealt with by the developing character. Sometimes the strength of a number can be a frustration when we're young.

If looking back on your own childhood through the lens of your number, you should discover — with considerable humour and irony — a renewed understanding of some of the difficulties or excitements you experienced. Or, if you have a child who is also a **3**, you may learn something more useful; it is an advantage to understand the qualities a number exudes over an awakening personality, especially in relation to talents and career strengths, as it might save a lot of frustrations. You'll be able to appreciate the positive traits, and handle negative ones more sympathetically.

Here, we take a detailed look at what it's like to be a child bearing your number. But what about the other numbers? Perhaps you have a child who is a **6**, and you'd like to know what that means? Or maybe you'd like to gain insight into friends' and siblings' childhoods, to see if it sheds any light on the people they have become today? A short profile is given for each number, along with advice for a **3** parent on dealing with other-number offspring.

Just as your own parents would have discovered when you were a child, the hardest thing with a **3** child is dealing with their nervous energy and insatiable curiosity, keeping them productively busy. **3**s love having many friends, so a childhood that deprives them of company limits their ability to blossom fully.

The young 3

A child born on the 3rd, 12th, 21st or 30th is always listening and looking — and asking questions that are impossible to answer! If you have a child who's a **3**, this means you're going to have an active little person on your hands. Asking a **3** child to sit still while you're busy doing something else is not realistic. Keeping them on the move — in a pushchair or in the car, or out somewhere on a day-trip — is your best hope of giving yourself thinking time while they wonder at the world that goes by.

And if you're hoping for smooth sailing when you take them visiting — crossing your fingers that they won't say the wrong thing, or let any cats out of proverbial bags — you will have a few surprises as the day unfolds. But, rather than attempting to gag your bright-eyed **3** — surely an impossible feat! — trust to their charm to say something amusing and get away with it stylishly. **3** children have a capacity to laugh and precipitate laughter, even when things go a little wrong; like the reappearing sun after rain, their energies can be restorative for everyone. Creative and playful, nothing keeps them low for long.

As the years pass by, parents of **3** children will have to up the voltage with their energy level, and it may prove tough going keeping up with them. Like a juggler keeping plates and balls in the air, **3**s have lots of activities and talents on the go from the start, but this can be a problem. Not only is it exhausting for the parents, but it can also be frustrating for the child. Making decisions is hard for them, and they need a wise older counsellor who can give them room to think and talk out the options. Even then, a decision once reached can always be changed – and a **3** child will find a way to run in several directions at one time.

From babyhood, **3**s should be kept busy with lots of artistic activities, using colours and textures to open their

3's toys

Art box • Camera (video and stills) • Dancing lessons • Microphone • Karaoke box • Music • Ice skates • Talking books • Sleepover kit • Colourful backpack • Joke book • Magic set • Whoopee cushion • Dressing-up chest

eyes to what they can do. Toys that incorporate colourful materials, each different to the touch, are perfect to help them develop their tactility and imagination. Even before they have reached the age of ten, they will have a strong personal taste developing – and it may not be the same as their parents'.

Using up their flow of energy on a multitude of tasks will be demanding of both parents, but the **3** child does give a lot back in return. Entertaining and full of fun, they are excellent mimics of everyone from their maiden aunt to their games teacher, and many times you will see a **3** child convert an adult's tears of sadness to those of laughter. **3**s make us forget ourselves for a while, and remember that the sun still shines somewhere. And they are very generous and giving.

3s are great talkers and have a witty repartee, even when very young: you'll be surprised at what you hear from them sometimes, and will wonder where it came from. Naturally gifted at PR, they will talk you around when you are set against one of their wishes, but you will need to direct them now and again or nothing will ever be finished!

A **3** parent with a **3** child should understand very well how much their young one needs freedom to experiment, and will not be upset if they are sometimes messy or chatter too much. If you are physically fit – a requisite! – and are always loving and kind, you will create a very strong and reciprocal bond with your **3** child. Don't worry if they rush about without much serenity: they have a way of using up their vitality on interesting creative projects, and, even when they pop their nose somewhere it may not be wanted, their charm and courage wins over most reluctant admirers. Through several brushes with near-danger, they will usually come back smiling.

The 1 child

This resourceful child has a different way of thinking, and will stand to one side and evaluate things without pressure. Repeat Grandma's sound advice on any subject to a **1** under the age of six, and they'll simply ask, 'Why?' Ignoring the social expectation to conform, **1** children often make us laugh with surprise.

A **1** child is tough and active – an inquisitive soul who wants to get on with things and not be held in check by others, however wise the parental eye might be. Stubborn and impatient, **1**s frequently suffer by questioning – though not from rudeness – the authority of a parent or teacher. **1**s break down tradition and find new ideas to form a fresh understanding of the world we're in. Your **1** child needs careful handling: a bright mind bursting with interest and disinclined to authority needs subtle direction. If **1** children dominate their friends and talk over their family it can make them socially inept and unable to co-operate in love relationships later in life, leading to loneliness rather than just self-reliance.

A **1**'s greatest challenge is to learn to live in a social world and understand that they are not inevitably right. To foster a **1**'s unique personality and avoid insensitivity to others, let them behave like an adult. This confidence a **1** child will ably repay. **1** children suffer from being misunderstood, as they're often so happy in their private hours and so demanding of having their own time that they may not learn to express their need for others. The seeds are sown early as to how to approach another person for signs of affection, and a loving **3** parent should easily tap-dance across a **1** child's innate sense of privacy, and bathe them in affection or reduce them to laughter. And they will relish your creative and warm approach.

2   1   9   8   7   6   5   4   3

The 2 child

All children born on the 2nd or 20th need affection and a peaceful environment to grow up in. Those born on the 11th or 29th are a little different, being master number **11**s with **2** as the denominator, and they have an old head on young shoulders from the beginning of their lives. But even they – for all their drive toward excitement and adventure – will be happiest if their home life is mostly secure and tranquil.

These highly sensitive and intuitive children know what you will say before you say it. They are also dreamy and process ideas in their sleep, waking to instinctive and wise solutions to their problems. But they are vulnerable, and need reassuring more than most numbers. They are acutely sensitive to criticism, feeling that all comments are proof that they're not quite good enough, so you need to deliver your words with tact and an awareness of their needs.

| 3 | 4 | 5 | 6 | 7 | 8 | 9 | 1 | 2 |

2 children are talented artists, actors, dancers and/or musicians: they know how others *feel*. A **2** child prefers to support friends and family as often as possible, and this can make them a doormat ready to be walked on unless those they live with are alert to their inclinations. If the **2** is an **11**, the wish to help out will be very strong indeed, but these children also have a finely tuned moral sense and will be offended by injustice – especially against them! Don't dish out judgement until you have all the facts.

All **2**s are good healers and can make others feel better – even from their earliest years. Knowing when to cuddle or touch and when to be quiet, they often have a stillness which works miracles around the sick, the sad and the elderly. A **3** parent with a **2** child must be careful not to talk across them, or neglect to give them quiet space for their inner calm. A **2** child has a very different style to yours, but **3** loves children, so it's unlikely you'll forget how much joy and support you receive from your gentle, intelligent **2**.

The 4 child

Surprisingly insecure and in need of praise, these children are reliable and hard-working and want to do well. They are their own worst critics at times, second only to number 7 children, and they glow when appreciated. They are happiest with family around them – even extended members – and often prefer holidays in familiar places. That said, they can be very quiet and self-sufficient when required, for they concentrate well.

These are organized children who won't cope well if their parents aren't as organized as they are! Never lose a school form or an item from their games kit on a crucial day, as this will cause them serious panic. They like to have material possessions around them because this bolsters their feeling of security, and will manage their pocket money well, content to do odd jobs and chores to gain this reward.

3   4   5   6   7   8   9   1   2

4s love the earth and buildings. They will treasure a patch of garden given them to tend, or a garden house they can extend or build outright. If they are born on the 22nd, rather than the 4th, 13th or 31st, they will truly have architectural talents, and may follow design as a career later. All **4** children, though, are handy at craft work and excellent at projects which require intelligence combined with method to get something done. They hate being late and don't admire tardiness in others, either.

As children, **4**s are loyal and dependable to family and friends, and are more patient than many numbers. They will make light of complex tasks, but they need to be allowed to do things in their own way. A **3** parent will be amused by their **4** child's method, and perhaps think them unimaginative; they simply have a different approach to life. **4**s feel responsible to others, which you'll encourage. Your energy is at odds with their stillness, but you respect their tenacity, and the relationship may grow into one of admiration.

2 1 9 8 7 6 5 4 3

The 5 child

Unable to be confined or to sit still, a **5** child is bursting with curiosity about life and people. Very sociable and happy to be on the move, these adventurous youngsters have much in common with **1**s, but are more willing to work in a team, and good at picking up on other people's ideas, only to improve them.

From their first few words, **5** children have good memories and a facility for speech – they speak and learn quickly, and can pick up more than one language. Even more physical than **1**s (although the two numbers are alike in this), they are excellent at sport or physical co-ordination. They chatter, are full of energy, and like to play to an audience. But most importantly, **5** children love to be free – to explore, laze, hunt, create, discover and travel. Take your **5** child away on holiday and they quickly make friends with others, and acquire a taste for foreign places. They will even experiment with different food, if you're lucky.

5s find a reason to slip away if they're bored with adult company — so don't be offended. Their minds can pursue several streams of active interest, so they need a great deal of amusement to stretch them. This adventurous spirit can be a worry to their family sometimes and, indeed, **5**s need to understand house rules about asking first, or telling someone where they're off to. The difficulty is that **5** children usually don't want to explain themselves to anyone.

The test for a **5**'s parent is to set their child constructive challenges that will vent their curiosity in good ways. **5**s will pick up technology and music (other forms of language, in a sense) quickly, but they don't like dull routine work — which will irritate a **4** sibling if they have one. A **3** parent of a **5** child will have much in common with their clever, restless offspring, but arguments about their freedom to roam may be a problem — even for you!

The 6 child

Here's a young soul in need of a peaceful haven, just like a
2, but a **6** will literally feel ill if there is dissension around
them. Always wanting to beautify their surroundings and
make pretty presents for Mum, these talented, sensitive
children have many gifts for creative expression. They will
also nurse the sick cat or anyone who needs gentle kindness, but are not always robust themselves, and should be
sheltered from bad weather or aggressive viruses.

As children, **6**'s musical talents should emerge – and
they often have beautiful speaking or singing voices. They
are also the peacemakers of the family – natural creators
of balance and harmony. Give them a free hand with their
bedroom and their flower garden, and be ready to learn
from them. Both boys and girls usually make good cooks
when they are older, too, so time spent in the kitchen won't

be wasted. Birthday presents that foster their good eye — a camera or set of art tools — will usually fit them well.

Despite being sensitive to others and quite intuitive, **6** as a child is a little shy and needs drawing out — especially if there has been much change in their young life, because **6** children need stability and like to remain a tiny bit traditional. They become very attached to their home. But if their family life is unconventional they will ultimately adjust, because they offer their family a lot of love, and like to be shown love in return. Even the boys have a feminine side, which in no way calls their gender into question.

Good at school and almost as well-organized as **4**s, this is a number which needs time to grow into itself: **6**s really are enormously talented. A **3** parent shares their **6** child's creative gifts and love of beauty, but must allow them some peace and calm. When you need a friend to listen, support, encourage and back *you* up, you will often find unsuspected reservoirs of strength in this interesting child.

2   1   9   8   7   6   5   4   3

The 7 child

Even in primary school this is a child with a focused mind and a strongly developed critical sense. A **7** child is perceptive and, sometimes, disarmingly quiet. They will often prefer adult company, as their peers will probably seem too young and underdeveloped to them. Wise and difficult to know well, these are children with a serious cast to their intelligent minds.

The fact that a **7** child can sit quietly and contemplate things deeply should not imply that they are introverted: quite the opposite. A **7** will grow into a very good host as long as the company appeals, and they have a lovely sense of humour, apparent from their earliest years – even if it does sometimes find expression at others' expense. They will rarely be rude, but certainly have a good understanding of all that has been said – and what has not been.

Listen to their impressions of the people they deal with!

All 7s as children have an inward reluctance to accept other people's ideas automatically — rather like 1s — but there is a special propensity to independence in a child born on the 16th. This is the number of someone who finds it difficult asking for what they want — someone who often feels as though they haven't been consulted as to their own wishes. And all 7s certainly have definite ideas about what to believe.

7 children should be told the truth on virtually all matters; they will know if they are being deceived, and will respect being treated as an adult in any case. A 3 parent may find their reserve and maturity unnerving, but will respect their 7 child's strength. Though different — a 7 child keen to retire into privacy and personal space — these two numbers appreciate each other somewhat, and a 7 child gives any parent much to be proud of, both academically and in terms of humanitarian feelings.

The 8 child

Here we have a young executive in the making. Even when they are still at school these children have a canny nose for what will make good business – and yet they are generous, hard-working and prepared to learn everything it will take to succeed in this life. Children born on the 8th, 17th and 26th like to have charge of their own finances, and to be given scope to do 'grown-up' activities – organizing their own parties and making arrangements for outings with their friends.

These children have strength and energy, but mentally are reflective and wise, too. They always see both sides to an argument – so parents who ask them to choose sides, beware! An **8** makes good judgements, and even before the age of ten they have a sense of what is fair and what is morally right.

3 4 5 6 7 8 9 1 2

As this number rules the octave, many **8** children are extremely musical and have a wonderful sense of rhythm. This last even assures they can be good at sport, as it takes innate timing to perfect many physical skills. **8**s also like philosophical ideas and relish being given 'big concepts' to chew over, especially concerning politics or religious ideas. **8**s are proud, and like to research things carefully – so as long as they are not bored, you will find an **8** child with their head in a book or on the internet, or watching programmes that educate and broaden their vistas.

An **8** child is always striving for balance, and you must be pragmatic if they are sometimes pulling in the opposite direction from you. **8**s are loyal to those they love, but a delicate sensibility makes them look at the other side of a story, or fight for an underdog. You understand this urge very well, and mostly you will respect the qualities and mind of your **8** child, who is as generous materially as you are.

2   1   9   8   7   6   5   4   3

The 9 child

Here is a person born for the theatre, or to travel the world and befriend everyone. 9s have an expansive view of things, and don't like to be restricted. With a good head for both science and the arts, there are many career directions a 9 may take, so parents will have their work cut out trying to help them choose. However, because the number 9 is like a mirror, with every number added to it reducing again to that same number (for example: 5+9 = 14, and 1+4 = 5), 9 children are able to take on the feelings of just about anyone, which is why they are so artistic and good at drama and writing.

From their first years in school it will be clear a 9 child has a wonderful dry sense of humour and a taste for the unusual. 9 children are not often prejudiced and seem to be easy-going – though they are sensitive to the atmosphere around them, picking up vibes like a sponge. If you speak to them harshly they will take it seriously, and are protective of others who seem to be hurt in this way too.

9s have a delicate relationship with their parents, but particularly with the father figure. A **9** girl will want to idolize her dad, and will feel desperately disappointed if circumstances are against this, while a **9** boy may wish to emulate his father – and yet they often grow up without enough input from this important person, who is busy or away. A **9** child must be wise ahead of their time, and so this lesson is thrown at them in one guise or another.

The **3** parent of a **9** child understands well how to go with the flow, allowing a stream of friends and interests through their door! Your **9** child appreciates your humour and warmth towards their friends, and recognizes your largesse of spirit, rewarding you with affection and kindness. Grown-ups from the start, their philosophical mind and willingness to keep the peace fills you with admiration.

2   1   9   8   7   6   5   4   3

3 AT PLAY

We have discovered how your number expresses itself through your character in relation to your family and your general personality, what instinctive reactions go with your number in everyday situations, and how it might shape your career path and colour your childhood. But every day our DAY number also influences the way we respond to the social world around us. So, what can it say about our leisure hours? Is yours a number that even allows itself to relax? (Well, you probably already have some answers to this one!) What can your number reveal about the way you like to spend your time, or how you achieve pleasure outside of duty?

3   4   5   6   7   8   9   1   2

Over the next few pages we take a look at what makes you tick, as a **3**, when you are unwinding – and how **3**s prefer to fill their time, if given a choice. Let's see whether you're typical in this respect ... And who knows – if you haven't already tried all the activities and pastimes mentioned, maybe you'll get a few ideas about what to put on your list for next time!

The 3 woman at play

If you have taken on board the salient points of a **3**'s character discussed so far, you may recognize a need both to be entertained by the world and to be entertaining *yourself*. A quiet life in the country is not a realistic dream for **3** — however much the idea might appeal! Yours is a world that must stimulate and challenge you, not demand permanent chill-out time away from the stresses of life.

Therefore, leisure for you is active, not idle. You will be happiest when you are relaxing and thinking at the same time, creating — or executing — artistic projects, planning gardens or home decoration, designing clothes or areas of your home. Leisure for a **3** is a chance to achieve personal goals or learn new disciplines, because life is simply never full enough to fit in all the things a **3** would like to do. And a **3** woman is sociable and generous with her friends, too,

| 3 | 4 | 5 | 6 | 7 | 8 | 9 | 1 | 2 |

so it's likely she needs to include others in her weekend plans. But what might they be? Is a relaxing weekend for you the same as for, say, one of your **2** girlfriends?

All you **3** girls start your weekend at five pm on a Friday: the minute work ends, the nail colour changes and the party shoes go on. If your partner is working late, you might declare a preference for 'just a quiet night with the girls' — meaning dinner and a movie, and even dancing, before getting home fresh as a daisy at one in the morning. How does anyone keep up? But there is no shortage of friends wanting to come along for the ride, for a **3** female companion makes everyone laugh and forget their woes from the first tequila.

Love is leisure for a **3** woman — and you are likely to be wildly creative in your love life! This, however, properly belongs in the section that follows, so let's skip over the lingering Saturday-morning breakfast in bed and get to the art class or hot-air-balloon trip you manage to squeeze in before lunch, which itself is taken on the hop – and rarely alone! Energy and vigour are the keynotes of **3**'s free time, and you can get through a mountain of activities without noticing. All your artistic talents come to the fore when you have a vacation, and a happy holiday is one which allows an activity like cycling with your family or partner – not to mention fabulous shopping. **3** shops for leisure, and has an eye for a bargain and a nose for a find!

If a **3** woman is forced to sit still and do some think-ing in her personal time – if a lover is away, for instance, or there is an emotional pause for some reason – she will sit and think while she is *doing* something: making jewellery, painting, writing. Seeing an end product from her leisure time helps **3** to think and regain control, and keeping busy is the way to deal with problems. Travel, therefore, is almost as desirable for the **3** female as it is for a **5**, and having pretty luggage and travelling at five minutes' notice is a happy option for the **3** woman with a sudden free weekend. City-breaks will appeal – combining shopping, colour and energy, as well as the chance to chat and find friends. **3** women never keep a broken heart for long before their ego is nursed back to health by an admirer found in the seat next to them on the plane, or on a bus stuck in traffic. **3**'s charm goes everywhere with her, turning leisure to business and business to pleasure.

There will never be enough time in life for you to perfect your surfeit of artistic gifts, but some talent for golf or jogging sits comfortably beside a love for opera or pop concerts, mosaic-making or baking, sketching or dancing. And, if the mood takes you – or if you are forced to be quiet for a time – your brain ticks over reading the newspaper or a book, or chatting on the phone. Your life is full, packed with such a variety of leisure activities that it is inconceivable for anyone to chronicle the possibilities. No one keeps up; and perhaps that's why you have so many very different – slightly oddball? – friends to go out with.

2   1   9   8   7   6   5   4   3

The 3 man at play

Fred Astaire in his prime could hardly slide and shuffle across so many platforms for his energies as a **3** man having fun! You certainly know how to enjoy yourself. With plenty of mates to keep you company – of both sexes and all ages – you're on the go from morning till late. Casual acquaintances beware: trying to out-drink, out-dance or out-talk a **3** man is not advisable, for you will laugh at them as you gulp down an evening-primrose capsule and pick up where you left off the night before. Not for the faint-hearted!

A **3** man can be happy anywhere. Like a snail, you take your favourite pleasures everywhere with you. You'll find friends in any bar or restaurant – even if they're people you've never met before – and will adopt a cast of motley characters that you'll find something in common with.

Social outings form a core of delight, and those who haven't known you outside work will be astonished by your ability to swing from chandeliers and make things happen everywhere. You will try anything at least once.

Travel, for a **3** man, is a leisure priority – but you will prefer a comfortable hotel or resort where you can luxuriate and appreciate its aesthetic qualities. You would rather take a lover or a friend along than go somewhere alone, but you will keep your travelling pal busy and pack in many delights. Make sure your companion knows not to expect any quiet evenings in: life is a playground for you, and the world is your oyster. They may also be advised to hold your imagination in check, after you've had a few glasses of firewater … if they don't want to find out whether you will stop short of outraging society! **3**'s taste is usually good, but you fear no reprimand at any time! Of course, bending a few rules, though, is part of your playtime.

2   1   9   8   7   6   5   4   **3**

3 gents have a range of leisure interests: sailing really appeals — for its colour and multiplicity of demands — as does any other activity which demands your excellent hand–eye co-ordination. Your rhythm makes you a natural tennis player or (when you want to role-play at lord of the manor) croquet opponent, and others shouldn't think that you'll be civilized about it, and let them win, either! **3** plays hard, and laughs hard afterwards, but you're probably a gracious winner and an even more gracious loser. Competition is important to the fun, though.

A **3** male host is at home with guests in his comfortable space, being a dab hand at cooking and a very amusing raconteur over lunch. Leisure is, thus, often time for having friends over — but if you invite them to share your table at Christmas, they must be prepared to leave their reticence behind and play charades or darts, or do a quiz, after the food. A **3** man expects everyone to be in the mood for stimulation rather than relaxation.

But the final word on a **3** taking advantage of their leisure time – male or female, for that matter – is to say that no list of suggestions can be close to the number of permutations a **3** will make. Sport, arts, travel, physical effort, hosting company, reading prolifically are the air that **3** breathes. **3** is a charming boy with a clever mind and a good heart. Heaven knows how many times in life he will surprise the people who know him very well.

Your romantic sense is properly a subject for the following section – but suffice to say it will not conform to standard expectation! You may amuse and delight your lover, but never behave as anticipated. The best recipe for happiness, from your partner's point of view, is for them to have no expectations of what you will do with your free time, as far as your love life is concerned. After all, anyone will tell you that what they love about a **3** (male or female) is their flexibility and lack of predictability – which is the one thing you will always be true to!

3 IN LOVE

Love: it's what we all want to know about. What's your style as a lover? And your taste — where does that run? Do you want a partner who is, ideally, as sociable and outgoing as you? Or would you rather have a love in your life who is happy to be quieter and let you take the lead, following along to share their discoveries with you at their own pace? Everything about you screams 'exuberance', but is this all there is to your love life?

Our first task is to consider how you see others as potential partners, and what you are likely to need from them. Why are you attracted to someone in the first place? This is where we begin ... But then you might like to pass the book across to your other half (if you have one), for the second subject of discussion is: why are *they* attracted to *you*? What does it mean to have a **3** lover?

Telltale traits of the 3 lover

- Exciting, sexy, good company
- Striking taste
- Likes their partner to look stylish
- Loves an active relationship
- Prefers a loyal partner who allows them a degree of freedom
- Surprisingly shy until they feel secure
- A flirt, but also honest in a relationship

2 1 9 8 7 6 5 4 3

How do you do?
A 3 IN ATTRACTION

A **3** shines in any social grouping – so being attractive to others comes easily for you. When *you* become interested in another is often when they stir your sparring instincts; tension and a little drama have a great sexual dynamic! You will be thrilled by anyone who can deliver a riposte to your witticisms, and communication is a vital part of your whole personality when you're in love. This makes you a wonderful conversationalist, and a good partnership for you emotionally will be with someone who is either an enthralled listener or, better still, an ideal blend of listener and contributor. The usual fascination for a **3** – or, rather, what provokes your attention the most – is when someone takes you on a little, argues the toss, as long as it is done with charm. A **3** in love always has grace, and will be magnetically drawn to anyone who exudes this same quality.

You are likely to be attracted to someone who is sexy and yet, possibly, not conventionally 'pretty' or beautiful by everyone's standards. In fact, you like to run the gamut and fall for someone who is a little bit dangerous or different. This is because you like a challenge in love, and yet also want more than just a lovely face to look at. A **3** in love is looking for something a little 'showbiz', and you will rate a sense of humour in a lover more highly than a well-paid job or traditional good looks. A **3** lives to be entertained – and entertain*ing* – and any partner who wants to tie or quieten you down is going to be in for a shock.

If you are feeling a strong pull towards someone, chances are that you'll win them over with your energy and 'infinite variety'! What draws others to you is also the challenge: **3** cannot easily be known fully. This is not because you are reticent or undemonstrative, like **1**, or deep and possibly wounded from your past, like **7**. It's because there is so much going on with a **3** that it is difficult for others to say when they have seen the 'true **3**'.

For their lovers, **3**s present so many paradoxes: bold and yet surprisingly cautious; bubbly and yet oddly dutiful; charismatic and at-ease socially, although occasionally conceited and careless; very flirtatious while strongly in need of loving loyalty. **3** is always on the move, changing smiles and clothes, finding new impulses and interests, aware of the need for financial sense and yet astonishingly spendthrift! This makes it tough for anyone in love with you to know when they have really touched your heart. It may take years for your partner to understand that you are happy with them and intend to be faithful, despite the fact that you relish the attention you still attract walking into a room and being admired. Flirting and being loyal to your love are not at odds for you. And, to be fair, you are usually happy when your partner attracts outside attention, too, not expecting that this will cause problems at home. Faithfulness and the freedom to be charming to others go hand in hand for a **3** – male or female, young or older. Others looking in from outside may not understand.

You're the one that I want

Love relationships are very important to you, and you will want a partner whom you feel you can spoil and have fun with. For this reason, **3**s often do get on best with those of a similar, buoyant nature – someone young at heart, with an idealistic spirit. Yet your inherent agelessness means you also need a lover who will quietly assume some responsibilities, and not be affected when you seem fragmented. It's a balancing act: you will work best with a partner you can lean on at times, and yet who allows you scope and time to find your own unique way of doing things.

3s often have unusual relationships – not the prescription laid down by society. It may be that you find love with someone markedly older – or younger – or of the same sex, or from a totally different social class or background. A **3** will love where it does, whether or not anyone outside understands. And even when you find a partner to be happy with who all the world approves of or endorses, it may be that your lifestyle choice won't be entirely conventional. **3** is never all that worried about the rule book! Nor should anyone try to advise a **3** whether a partner is or is not the right one: interference will almost certainly backfire!

So what is a **3** really looking for in love? This isn't such a mystery. You would be elated with a partner who intuits your needs; someone who steps back a little to give you social sway, and yet stands just behind you offering support. Someone who has enough wisdom to weather your moods and know when you are just temporarily stressed and grumpy. A lover who has humour and resilience – who doesn't take you too seriously when you're only playing with an idea or another person in an argument. You definitely blossom when you are beloved, and you need to feel truly desired by another person — not just that you're filling in time. You must be the passion that exhausts them.

And what's going to excite you in a partner? You admire the charm and social ease that you know you draw yourself, but you may respect old-fashioned romantic gestures, which will surprise many. Secretly you like romance, and, although an exhilarating physical relationship is a buzz, you love to be surprised and have a chase on your hands. You need to keep moving and have to try new things with a loved one yourself — someone who stretches you and brings out your best charm and affability is your soulmate. This person needs to let you feel you have the limelight in the relationship, and at the same time be strong and dependable for you. **3**, remember, is a lovely child, and never completely grows up; your partner may need to be enchanted by this, and yet take the quiet lead in day-to-day banalities. **3**s, perhaps, ask a lot — but they give a lot, too!

To have and to hold?

LOVING A NUMBER 3

If you are in love with a **3**, you have chosen a relationship that's like a Ferris wheel: great highs and strange lows. Love will be entertaining, as will life. At the top, the rest of the world seems small and insignificant, and everything else takes second place to the butterflies in the tummy your **3** produces. You may never know in conventional words how loved you are, but will have to take this on trust. If your **3** pampers and cossets you, you know you have inspired that strong, deep feeling. Your lover will charm and infuriate you, deny you certainties about anything, and yet fascinate and inspire you to want a life of any and all possibilities. Together, you won't settle for banality or stifling security: true high-flyers, you will soar into the clouds and roll with the times when things inevitably

| 3 | 4 | 5 | 6 | 7 | 8 | 9 | 1 | 2 |

change and put you through some tougher periods. But, if you love a **3**, this is the stuff of life!

You will be proud of your **3**'s social ease, love their way of making an entrance and keeping a table of strangers enthralled by their own sense of merriment. You love their facile manner of talking and finding topics of interest for all; and you may see them as being like the sun, lighting up the atmosphere and drawing others to rotate around them. It is impossible not to admire your **3**'s way of bringing optimism to people who are low; of getting them to try something new. Your **3** love is popular, and has a fertile imagination: who would be with anyone else?

Let's get physical ...

There's no denying that a great sex life features around a **3**: if you love one, you know how imaginative they are behind closed doors! A **3** will make you laugh and cry in

2   1   9   8   7   6   5   4   **3**

bed, and this forms an important part of your intimacy. If the physical relationship ever completely goes, there may be trouble in paradise. Staying fit and making a priority of private time between you is a prerequisite for a happy relationship, as is the willingness to enter into **3**'s playful and exuberant moods. Your **3** is clever and vivacious, but also a willing accomplice to anything not in the script. If you can keep one step ahead of them, your relationship will benefit substantially.

It's important to recognize that your **3** lover is a people person — indeed, you probably love them because of that extroverted popularity and vitality. But you must be honest enough to admit that there will be times this causes jealousy for one or both of you, and that you may become irritable if you find your **3** unnecessarily flippant or conceited. Always give them space to shine without feeling ignored yourself, and, if you can do this, you may have just what it takes to make you both happy for a long time.

3   4   5   6   7   8   9   1   2

Equally, it will help if you understand that your **3** is a loyal person underneath, and that flirtations are not alternative relationships! The courtship path may not be straightforward – for there is always more than one person in the equation with a **3**. This may be someone from the past, an admirer, an unfinished love relationship. Complications are the norm, and the one who wins **3**'s heart is the one who can stand at ease with themselves through all of this. If this is not for you, quit early before your heart takes a pounding – but keep it in mind that once a **3** makes a choice, loyalty and true love are profoundly possible. It's just that a faint heart, perhaps, never won a fair **3**!

3 in love

Turn-ons:
- ♥ ✔ A lover with a sense of humour and a good ear
- ♥ ✔ Someone who won t try to change your youthful zest for life and need for variety
- ♥ ✔ A person with a good brain, kind heart and independent personality, who dresses with flair
- ♥ ✔ Someone for whom sex life is equally important: sex is key!

Turn-offs:
- ♥ ✘ A cloying partner who resents intrusions from others socially
- ♥ ✘ Someone who is mean-minded about money and unappreciative of your generosity and taste
- ♥ ✘ Anyone who tries to tie you down or bring up your past to haunt you
- ♥ ✘ Someone who is too much of a loner

3'S COMPATIBILITY

In this weighty section you have the tools to find
out how well you click with all the other numbers
in matters of the heart, but also when you have to
work or play together too. Each category opens with
a star-ratings chart, showing you – at a glance –
whether you're going to encounter plain sailing or
stormy waters in any given relationship. First up is
love: if your number matches up especially well with
the person you're with, you will appreciate why
certain facets of your bond just seem to slot
together easily.

But, of course, we're not always attracted to the people
who make the easiest relationships for us, and if you find
that the one you love rates only one or two stars, don't

give in! Challenges are often the 'meat' of a love affair — and all difficulties are somewhat soothed if you both share a birthday number in common, even if that number is derived from the *total* of the birth date rather than the actual **DAY** number. In other words, if your partner's **LIFE** number is the same as your **DAY** number, you will feel a pull towards each other which is very strong, even if the **DAY** numbers taken together have some wrinkles in their match-up. You will read more about this in the pages that follow the star chart.

The charts also include the master numbers **11** and **22**: these bring an extra dimension to relationships for those whose birth-number calculations feature either of these numbers at any stage. (For example, someone with a **DAY** number of **2** may be born on the 29th: 2+9 = **11**, and 1+1 = **2**. This means you should read the compatibility pairings for your number with both a **2** and an **11**.)

Sometimes the tensions that come to the surface in

love relationships are excellent for business relationships instead: the competitiveness that can undermine personal ties can accelerate effectiveness in working situations. We'll take a look at how other numbers match up with yours in vocational situations. And, when it comes to friends, you'll see why not all of your friendships are necessarily a smooth ride ...

In all matters – whether love, work or friendship – you will probably discover that the best partnerships you make involve an overlap of at least one number that you share in common. A number **3** attracts other number **3**s in various close ties throughout life.

NOTE: To satisfy your curiosity, **ALL** numbers are included in the star charts, so that you can check the compatibility ratings between your friends, co-workers and loved ones – and see why some relationships may be more turbulent than others!

2   1   9   8   7   6   5   4   3

Love

YOUR **LOVE** COMPATIBILITY CHART

	1	2	3	4	5
With a 1	★★★★	★★★★★	★★	★★★	★★★★★
With a 2	★★★★★	★★★★	★★★	★★★★★	★
With a 3	★★	★★★	★★★★★	★★	★★★★
With a 4	★★★	★★★★★	★★	★★★★	★★
With a 5	★★★★★	★	★★★★	★★	★★★
With a 6	★★★	★★★★	★★★★	★★★	★★
With a 7	★★★★★	★★	★★★	★★★★★	★★★
With an 8	★★★★	★★★★	★★★★★	★★★	★★★
With a 9	★★★	★★★	★★★★★	★★	★★★
With an 11	★★★★	★★★★	★★	★★★★★	★★
With a 22	★★★★	★★★★★	★★★	★★★★	★★★★

3   4   5   6   7   8   9   1   2

6	7	8	9	11	22
★★★	★★★★★	★★★★	★★★	★★★★	★★★★
★★★★	★★	★★★★	★★★	★★★★	★★★★★
★★★★	★★★	★★★★★	★★★★★	★★	★★★
★★★	★★★★★	★★★	★★	★★★★★	★★★★
★★	★★★	★★★	★★★	★★	★★★★
★★★★★	★	★★★	★★★★★	★★★★	★★★★
★	★★★	★★★★	★★★	★★★★	★★★★★
★★★	★★★★	★★★	★★	★★★★★	★★★★
★★★★★	★★★	★★	★★★	★★★★	★★★
★★★★	★★★★	★★★★★	★★★★	★★	★★★★★
★★★★	★★★★★	★★★★	★★★	★★★★★	★★

2 1 9 8 7 6 5 4 3

3 in love with a 1   ★★

In friendship, this connection between the creative juices of the **3** and the **1**'s originality and spark is very good: you sing to the same tune. But, in love, this relationship can be exhausting. **1** is attracted to your energy and charm, and, very often, to your physical good looks – **3**s tend to be among the best-looking of the numbers! However, there can be a little competition here, with regard to both of you being important and in the limelight, and **3**'s personal magnetism can be a *bête noire* for **1** sometimes. You are not so much cut from the same cloth as cut from equally showy, fine-quality cloth of different kinds!

Certainly, your flamboyant **1** will never bore you, and what does work is that you both love to pack your lives with action and *doing*. You are creative, love the arts, and keep finding interests that appeal to you both. However, as a **3** you expect to be the star in a very humorous – even child-like – way, which will occasionally irritate self-interested **1**. Also, your **1** may find your inability to focus on any one thing to the exclusion of others really infuriating. When **1** goes into a mindset to achieve something, nothing will distract them until all the notes are composed in their head, as it were, and recorded on the page. Then, admittedly, they will delegate the concerto to someone else's hands – the conductor, who will see it through to performance. As a **3**, though, you may have too many opuses on the go, and your **1** could feel (with some justification!) that nothing ever moves past the ideas stage.

You can also be very indecisive, which can even be a problem at the outset of the attraction between you. Self-absorbed – though fascinating – your **1** knows what they want and what they like, and will want to get on with things and start exploring your manifold personality. But tantalizing **3** has a tendency to run hot and cold early on in attraction, and it can be confusing for anyone. You are often unable to make up your mind as to what you want. It's this person today, and someone else tomorrow. This is not fickle, but more that you are truly undecided about what works, and it will drive **1** – who is used to being the centre of attention – mad. It may seem to them as though you can't be loyal – or be trusted.

If you have another number in common, the more positive aspects of the relationship can shine out. This means that the two of you work in synthesis, **1** handling one set of needs and **3** probably doing PR for them, while **1** gets the ball rolling and helps you to put your dynamic energies behind something – effectively making up your mind for you. This can help you both to exude a certain gloss and showbiz glamour about you as a pair. When you combine your talents, the sky is the limit.

Trouble comes when **1** makes selfish demands, or you make **1** doubt themself – or when you inadvertently scatter **1**'s attention and drive. A **1** can be impulsive, and this makes you nervous. What's more, when your chatterbox tendency comes to the fore, and you can't sit still or keep quiet, you deny your 1 their vital private space. Together, you will have to decide how big a problem this is; but it will cause you some frustrations not infrequently!

Key themes

Excellent hosts · Many friends · Good energies · Variety in life together, but often a retreat into individual selfishness and lack of understanding

3 in love with a 2   ★★★

These two numbers are attracted to each other physically – very much so. **3** has an energy and vitality that appeals to tranquil **2**, being so different from **2**'s own love of gentleness and quietude. You seem so sparky and confident, so alluring and young at heart, while **2** seems – to you – so still and serene, so grown up and caring towards other people. And you are definitely attracted by **2**'s physical beauty and good taste – even though it's not your own kind of taste. So, the sexual tension is likely to be sizzling for a while – but only for a while! After some time passes, problems will inevitably settle in ...

These two numbers have very different expectations of life, and different energies. It is not beyond possibility that this relationship could work – partly because the attraction is so strong. But difficulties arise in the day-to-day harmony. As a **3**, you may feel **2** is too staid and conservative in their whole approach to life, while **2** may feel (with reason) that you lack inner focus and seriousness about life. **3** is, by twists and turns, both marvellously free of social constraint and ridiculously immature. When things are fine, it will be the former, but when troubles set in ... So, not a marriage made in heaven, but it does have energy, and there is a chance it can work if **2** exercises full patience and you can respect their need for calm now and again!

Certainly, **2** appreciates your glamour and charisma, and together you are sure to be popular and have a wide variety of friends. You will get on with young and old, and all will be welcome at your table. Also, there is a chance of the two of you being very lucky with money – **2** knowing how to win over difficult customers with sheer tact and charm, and you being able to clinch the deal with wit and spontaneous actions. Another bonus is that **2** is not unhappy to take a secondary position in your life, to be the adviser, the aid, the support, while you thrill and entertain, and juggle lots of interesting options in the air.

In the end, it comes down to compromise. As a **3**, you must be sensitive to those moments when your **2** needs to spend time one on one, without a visiting circus. You also have to ask or encourage your **2** to give things a chance – rather than judging whether something will be wrong a priori. Maybe you can entice **2** into letting go of some of their fears and vulnerabilities; and perhaps **2** can persuade you to stand still long enough to listen to what they have to say. **3**s so often fend off serious discussion with an appearance of humour or being disinterested, so **2** may need to gently ask you to evaluate things more realistically sometimes.

So you see, this is a seesaw where the tempo and good feeling may be up one day and down the next. This is not necessarily a bad thing, for it may help **2** to learn just how flexible and conciliatory they can be. And you, **3**, may learn that there are some issues in life worth taking seriously: you aren't stupid, and have a quick, acute mind – if you would only apply it! It will be a challenge to make this partnership work, but not an impossibility. Patience will be the key – a key that **2**, perhaps, holds more than you?

If you have another number in common, the more positive aspects of the relationship will be able to emerge, and this will make a big difference. Equally, if you have many 'B's or 'T's in your name, this will give you more tolerance of **2**'s sensitivities. And, of course, the sensuality you share will be a huge plus.

Key themes

Smouldering mutual attraction thanks to different but complementary styles • Very good friendship with many people • Financial and social luck together • Love affair of highs and (very often!) lows

2   1   9   8   7   6   5   4   3

3 in love with a 3   ★★★★★

Two matching numbers together is often a recipe for dis-
aster, with all the faults doubling and neither partner being
able to see an alternative point of view. Not so for two **3**s!
Potentially, this partnership is excellent – although it may be
an exhausting courtship, and both of you will play strange
games at the start. **3**s, however, understand and are fired
by each other. You share the same wicked sense of humour,
have a mutual feeling for fun and the balance of pleasure
that life should contain, and you are vitally quite free with
one another. Moreover, because you entertain each other
so comprehensively, you seem to bring out the best in one
another, each inspired to greater and greater heights. Quite
simply, 3+3 = 6: and **6** is the number of love.

Together you take on the drab world around you with
humour and energy. Never letting a down day get the

3   4   5   6   7   8   9   1   2

better of you if you can party into the night, two **3**s have unassailable gumption – that pluck that makes the difference between surviving and caving in when things get tough. Your attraction to one another is obvious: you both want a relationship that entices, charms, challenges and entertains one another. And you both have a desire not to let things stagnate – even if you grow old and have twenty grandchildren together. Horizons beckon, and you both set sail into them, unafraid of unknown circumstances, ready to charm the world ... and each other. You have discovered that laughter is a remedy for almost every ailment.

There are dangers, of course. You both like to take chances and live life to the full. You believe in – and make your own – luck, and this takes you to some danger zones where things may get out of hand. Maybe you sometimes take things too far – flirtations, financial expenditure, emotional games? Neither of you is likely to caution the other one when your imagination becomes too eccentric or your ideas too expansive. Literally, life knows no bounds. And wastefulness is a problem, when the amazing opportunities you dream up fall on barren ground, since neither partner knows how to cultivate just one plan alone and see it through. You both keep so many possibilities in the air, and perhaps don't reveal exactly what is on your mind. Are you expecting the other person to do too much guesswork?

This, though, is the cautionary tale; and, while it has a place, it shouldn't eclipse the fact that you have huge resilience as a pair, and great appreciation for each other's flexibility. Being flexible in one's attitudes and approaches to life is perhaps the most valuable asset in any personality, for it means that coping with change and taking alternate directions when necessary is not back-breaking. If you are able to move with the times or adjust to circumstances, or find another direction to take when a gamble doesn't pay off, then you will come through anything. As long as you can play down some of the childish tendencies you may have at times, or the unwillingness to be responsible, you can tackle – and succeed at – any venture.

And let's face it: you'll have great fun as you run along together – attractive shared living space, one of you embarking on a creative course, cooking well for each other, unusual friends passing through your lives, adventures travelling into strange realms, and so many beautiful things decorating the edges of your day-to-day world. Plus, the physical relationship may be one thing that never goes off the boil, even when other elements are misfiring. With another **3** you share a comfort zone and a life that finds sunshine, even on cloudy days. Can you ask for more?

Key themes

Both watch the world go by from the fast lane • Great sex • Lots of laughter • Take many gambles together • Mostly both very lucky

2   1   9   8   7   6   5   4   3

3 in love with a 4   ★★

This is a strange relationship – quite possibly too dull for you in the long run. The only way you could make this relationship even progress beyond the starting blocks is to compromise with each other on a number of crucial points. Your world views are so different – **4** wanting security and a planned rhythm and direction, **3** wanting as much spontaneity as possible in every sphere (so, just the opposite!). **4** is the epitome of tradition, **3** the very flavour of change and modernism. **3** builds castles in the air and **4** utility rooms; **3** landscapes the Hanging Gardens of Babylon, and **4** a vegetable garden. The **4** is cautious with money, and the **3** completely undisciplined. And, where the **4** likes a physical relationship to take place in a clean and properly made bed, the **3** is planning something more risky – and only as the mood takes them. One number is

3   4   5   6   7   8   9   1   2

about preparation in life and the best-made plans, while the other is about seizing the most nebulous opening for fun.

There may be only a little friction between you, but the **4** will feel aggrieved by what they see as **3**'s flagrant disrespect for carefully arranged appointments and plans. Why are you late? Where have you been? How much have you had to drink? Not questions guaranteed to enchant a **3**. And actually, some of these questions may be fair enough. It's clear you have differing agendas. But what is most difficult is that a **4** may not express these differences openly, keeping them to themselves and brewing towards a showdown which seems over the top or out of proportion when it comes. **3** wonders what all the fuss is for. But **4** is naturally conservative and economical, where **3** is free-thinking and at least a little irresponsible. What can possibly have attracted two such people to each other?

The explanation is that opposites (and you are complete opposites!) do, of course, attract. **3** is so fascinated

2 1 9 8 7 6 5 4 3

by **4**'s sense of system and apparent maturity, and **4** is captivated by the fact that anyone can be so popular and easy-going, so lucky without apparent cause, so young and unafraid. But **3**'s love of luxury and expansiveness is just the thing to make **4**'s heart beat too fast – bordering on panic. Your best qualities clash with each other.

The only possible way forward is if you allow your dependable **4** to feel secure, and simply agree to embellish their stable, architect-built world. You would have to turn your creative eye to solid, investment-conscious projects. And **4** would need to loosen up, listen to your imaginative ideas and refuse the urge to quash them right from the word go. At best, you might show each other the way to create brilliant plans and give them a real foundation – to make dreams into actualities. But both of you would have to make big concessions and act, frankly, out of character.

I have my doubts as to how this could materialize – which is a shame, because in truth you need each other to let go of the less positive aspects of your characters. **4** could take on such a protective role with you, and you could feel **4**'s reliability as a plus. You also understand that **4** will not compete with you or take the limelight away from you. Your **4** enjoys the past, so if you design a modern space with lots of antiques you may please each other. **4** loves the country and you the water, so, again, perhaps you can find a way to blend the two? As long as you can get to the city quickly for some after-hours fun, of course!

Key themes

Shared pride in children (if it gets that far!) • Different values: **3** happy-go-lucky and **4** a careful planner • Creativity must be married with solid ideas if partnership is to work • **3** could unlace **4**'s rigidity • **3** dominates, while **4** is anchor

2   1   9   8   7   6   5   4   3

3 in love with a 5   ★★★★

There are many overlapping qualities between these numbers, which share a love of life and a zany sense of humour. **3** can't help being attracted to **5** for their brilliance and energy. Each is a variant of the other – different shapes cut from the same cloth, perhaps. **5** excites **3**'s vivid imagination, and both of you enter into word-play and behavioural chess games which indicate to others the degree of tangible sexual attraction. Next to a relationship with a **3** or an **8**, this is the best bond you might find with another person.

5 has notched up a little more experience than you in many respects, so what attracts each of you to the other is the opportunity to broaden each other's world. **5** loves to show eager and witty **3** how to shine in foreign places; and **3** makes **5** feel young and sexy all the time. You have a way of seeing the world – **5** in a funny but cynical man-

3	4	5	6	7	8	9	1	2

ner, and **3** in a pithy but normalizing way. Neither of you waits for a better opportunity to come if a door opens and a chance arises to be spontaneous. 'Pack your bags,' you might tell each other, or, 'Try it now!' Neither of you needs a second invitation to anything much!

5 is naturally very sexy and attractive in the eyes of a **3**; **5** is perhaps the only number to be more comfortable with their sexuality than you! You are drawn to their charm, style and colour – for **5**s never lead a dull life. Physical compatibility, for a **5**, is more than just a bonus if it happens: it is an essential ingredient in a good relationship. You won't argue with this, and the sensuous side of your relationship together will play an anchoring role in keeping you interested in one another. But is there more than sex?

Certainly! Two numbers who speak well, think fast, love to dip their toes in the water of life are bound to get on. You are both tolerant of almost anything and anyone, which is something that can make or break many other relationships. If you are broad-minded and generous to others mutually, it makes for a better starting point. Also important is the fact that **5** likes to get on with things, just as you do. It doesn't take days for your bouncy **5** to act on an idea, nor does it take you more than a moment to try something if it feels right. You love water, and **5** mountains – so you will meet each other for spontaneously planned rendezvous in both landscapes. **5** loves oriental food and bubbly champagne, and you love almost all good food and champagne – no conflict there. **5** is an outdoors person who dons the right attitude when the sun comes out; **3** always loves the sunshine and has a permanently tolerant view of a hot day. Bliss!

The relationship works best when both of your fine minds have been well-educated, which offsets a tendency to run at tangents just for the sake of excitement. Neither of you is necessarily deeply philosophical, but **5**'s electric mind is more inspired by your imaginative gifts and sense of optimism. You come up with such innovations, and **5** knows how to take them to the marketplace. This might strictly be business, but as you are uplifted by mental endeavour it can be very important in a daily routine that you respect, admire and promote each other's work lives. **5** is a hippy, perhaps, or a poet sometimes, but can often be a wasted talent; and **3**'s clever ideas also evaporate if there is no one to encourage and shape them. Oddly enough, you do this for each other.

Key themes

Both love freedom, which could create odd tense moments • Both have a strong sense of daring – especially sexually • Both prepared to find out how to satisfy the other • Shared humour a real feature of the attraction

3 in love with a 6 ★★★★

There are many good prospects for happiness in this romance, where two naturally creative people, full of kindness towards others, can make each other very happy. **6** has the substance to help **3** find an outlet for their artistic ability, and **3** draws the sometimes over-serious **6** into more laughter and joy in life. **3**, in fact, may help **6** to be more at ease with the idea of putting their own interests to the fore, as **6** so often retires into a feeling of what is duty. Also a problem is **6** thinking things through too much in life, and not putting their considerable talents behind a dream – but you will help remedy this. **3** and **6** marry congeniality and a love of people with a flair for synthesizing what is beautiful. This should appeal to both parties.

    3 loves **6**'s grace and elegance, which is sometimes a character trait as much as a style, and **6** is always appre-

3	4	5	6	7	8	9	1	2

ciative of **3**'s ease and sociability. Together these numbers find harmony in myriad ways: similar tastes in music and the arts, a willingness to support each other through personal goals, a feeling of pleasure in shared pledges towards friends and family. **6**, perhaps, even has the advantage of keeping **3** calmer, and **3** of exciting **6** into action when they might well prefer to sit back and let others steal their thunder. If **6** is afraid to self-promote, a **3** in love with them will happily do it for them.

You may become a shade less aggressive in company with your **6**. That aggression so often stems from nervous energy and insecurity about your emotions, but **6** offers you more inner tranquillity. Also, gentle **6** may help you to think about the future more, to ask yourself where you want to be a few years from now, helping you to plan and make the most of your exceptional talents. You are so used to being capable of so many things, yet failing to capitalize, and **6** will not only see your potential but glow with pride over your unique qualities, making you more aware yourself of what you have going for you. Life gets better when someone has true faith in you, which your sensitive **6** certainly does.

Your powerful optimism helps make cautious **6** believe more in the potential of life. A **6** in love is always happier, because this number needs an outlet for its natural affections, but somehow **6**s feel life throws burdens and responsibilities at us all to a greater extent than pleasure. You, though, have a knack for turning this pessimism away. Reminding **6** of all that is beautiful in life, you help them to loosen up with others and laugh – and the sound of a **6** laughing is magical. This sense of being needed may deepen the bonds between you. And, as a **6** is always worrying about that apocryphal 'rainy day', they help you to organize your money and accumulate more than usual, gently chiding if your wastefulness becomes too detrimental.

And what about your love style together? A **6** demands

3   4   5   6   7   8   9   1   2

– and gets – your loyalty more than anyone can, and keeps you on track for romance. Such a natural flirt, you often give others the impression that you can't settle. With a **6**, though, you'll want to make a beautiful nest and look after them. Gender becomes irrelevant, and, even if your **6** is younger than you, they will make you feel young, confident and desirable ... all of which means this relationship could go the distance, and make you both very happy for many, many years.

Key themes

Each of you wants company • Both fond of pleasure, and enjoy the same kinds of hobby • **6** gives **3** confidence, and **3** makes **6** laugh • The good feeling you generate brings financial luck

2   1   9   8   7   6   5   4   3

3 in love with a 7   ★★★

The one way that this relationship might work is if **3** agrees to be guided by **7**'s higher concentration span. You both have very agile minds, though **7** likes to focus on one thing to the exclusion of others until results come, while you dip and dive like a swallow into any number of interesting pursuits – not always bothering to achieve anything substantial. The chase is everything for **3**, but **7** can't tolerate such an inept use of intelligence. Maybe **7** will encourage you to keep your focus until you see your ideas through to a conclusion?

But, of course, this is important for a love relationship only if it is going to last, and not all relationships are about that. From the point of view of sheer attraction, the **7** is attracted to the **3** for their undoubted glamour and funny lines, while **3** admires a **7**'s skill in just about everything.

| 3 | 4 | 5 | 6 | 7 | 8 | 9 | 1 | 2 |

3 almost looks up to **7** – but this is not to say that **3** would like to *be* **7**. You are two different people – marvellous tennis players with very contrasting (and not necessarily well-suited) styles. **3** zips and splashes over a fast grass court with dashing footwork, whereas **7** out-thinks their opponent on a clay court by manoeuvring them into submission, taking much longer to gain the prize. **7** has more reliability in all things, but **3** finds this frustrating after the initial gloss has worn off. Besides, that strange **7** is always wanting to go off in solitude somewhere, while you have the telephone under your chin and are chatting online at the same time. Little agreement on the social mores of the relationship will also cause combat.

Plus, **7**'s motto of 'still waters run deep' won't necessarily appease **3**'s 'need to know' on most daily things. **3** is used to sharing and bouncing ideas off others, growing in the process and developing newer and even fresher ideas over time. **7** is too wise to give away their own thoughts to others like this, and also very mystical, whereas **3** is canny and sharp. Of course, this could be a wonderful marriage of opposites, so that you gain, in **7**'s higher interests, an outlet for your own brilliance – the **7** effectively drawing you out and showing you what you're capable of, if you can be decisive and apply your mind to something demanding for longer periods. **3** is intuitive, and aware instinctively of how people feel and what they need. But **7** will feel like darkness and light to sunny **3**, and however much attraction there is some of the time, for a serious relationship there are bound to be difficulties.

Sharing a common number would help hugely – if either of you has a common LIFE number, for instance (*see page 214*). Also, if you have the letters G, P or Y in your name, you will have a greater tolerance for **7**'s qualities of stillness and privacy. Essentially, however, this is a relationship that would demand greater compromise than either of you probably wants to make. Enjoy it as a fling, but be

3   4   5   6   7   8   9   1   2

ready to move on when the urge takes you! The fact that **7** never takes you seriously, and never seems to laugh except ironically, may be more than you can handle.

Key themes

Excellent minds of different ilk • Emotional needs not addressed • Respect for each other's differences (but problems because of them) • Better as business partnership, as can borrow from each other's contrasting talents

3 in love with an 8   ★★★★★

These numbers work in every possible situation! Whether you met over a drink at work, or on a train going away for a weekend, **3** and **8** are immediately comfortable with one another. You share hope, see the glass half full instead of half empty, and have the kind of positivity that makes people around you feel confident trusting in your dreams. Neither of you is so serious that you fail to see the ironies of life ... yet you each have a perceptive, generous nature.

What makes an **8** magnetic for a **3** is their far-reaching vision. While **3** looks behind the mask of everyone they meet and, in so doing, breaks down social barriers, **8** looks deep into the soul, and understands others' woes. Bringing these visions together gives you the potential as a pair to be happy in your hearts with one another, but also successful if you work together. **8** may not have your visual agility,

3   4   5   6   7   8   9   1   2

and will trust your taste for a final verdict on what looks good decorating a room (or themselves!), but is creative in ways you respect, having a powerful ability to move people with stirring words, which blends nicely with your wit and charm. And **8** is musical – seriously musical. Together you make a cheery tune to which you can dance through life.

Sometimes **8** is so busy looking ahead that they fail to see the pleasures under their nose; you help them correct this oversight. And, when you are just too frenetic or buried in the undergrowth to identify a problem or future direction, **8** cuts through the long grass and sees the way. You have such good ideas and communicative skills, and **8** has the drive and considerable power to make good these concepts. Together, these numbers reach high and low – and everything in between. This leads to some fascinating discoveries and world-changing discussions!

But what **3** loves personally about **8** is their style, their cache in the social world, the sense that they have made it to the top from nothing. **3** sees **8**'s vulnerabilities and yet applauds their courage in the face of difficulty; and, while **8** is soul-searching, **3** clowns around and helps them through.

Physically, this is a blending of quite sensuous energies. **8** is very physical, and **3** likes to create an environment for pleasure, which helps **8** to unwind. You will often remind **8** that it is important to have fun in life, and bring them into a social landscape where they will then emphatically win hearts and make a huge impression on others. This is remedial for **8**, for — regardless of gender — as a number it is apt to encounter tangles in work and responsibility. Also, while **8** is the number of serious money and corporate strength, it has runs of fortune, and may have to start again many times in business. You have the everyday luck to help them over each bad patch.

But what of high-minded **8**'s attraction to **3**? Why so strong? You have levity and yet, beside this, real insight.

No one may reduce **8** to tears of sensitivity more than you. **8** works and struggles, creates a sway in the world and makes an impact. Very often, a **3** is somewhere keeping them going. In a love relationship you can bring affection and joy without being too demanding, because your own number is sociable enough in such a variety of places that your partner doesn't always have to be the centre of your focus. This pairing is therefore potentially dynamic and highly compatible. You supplement each other's skills and desires, and know when to leave each other a little space. After the initial attraction has run its course, real love could well be in the air for you two.

Key themes

3 buoys **8** when **8** is under siege financially or in business • **3** believes in **8**'s real worth • Together, sociable and far-seeing • **3** helps **8** laugh; **8** makes **3** excel in what they do

2   1   9   8   7   6   5   4   3

3 in love with a 9   ★★★★★

This relationship has class and scope for durability. **9** loves everything and everyone, and **3** invites the sometimes moody **9** into the world to play a little more often. If there is one special gift you bring to a **9**, it's optimism, for **9** is very often brought down by others' social flaws. **3** rolls with the punches far better, and has a very uplifting effect on **9**, which is vital. You also have many things in common. You are drawn to **9**'s long list of talents and interests – in theatre and art, with words, with sounds. **9** broadens your vision, makes you feel there are real possibilities in this world. This is good for you, because your awareness, though sharp, is often limited by what is familiar, and **9** will make you much more desirous of knowing a greater world.

Problems can arise if **9** becomes too negative, because you really have little time for gloom. **9** is a mirror number, and reflects others strongly, losing its own identity and sense of self in the process. This isn't a problem if they are surrounded by bright spirits and laughing characters like you, but if your highly intelligent **9** has a bad day at work you'll wonder why it brings them so low, and why they can't just get over it. Nothing is quite so simple for a **9** – they may make heavy weather of things that you'd simply shrug off. Also, **9** may be too sensitive to criticism for your liking.

This is just a brief caution, however. If you love your **9**, be prepared to get through some rainy days; they won't be year-long, and **9** is a number well able to listen to reason over time. If you can be patient, you should find you can soon recover their personal sunshine, and emerge together into warmth again. And this is well worth doing, because **9** sees much more in you than others allow. The trouble with being known as the class clown is that your sensitivities and pains are either dismissed or ignored. **9** knows how you are inside, and helps you redirect disappointment and follow your dreams to fruition. In fact, no one does this better – for **9** sees real talent in your creativity.

In love you may be idealistic together, for there is a dreamy quality you share. **9** needs to get you to concentrate on financial order, and to maximize your considerable earning potential through your gifts – which **3**s often fail to do themselves. But your gentle **9** is a co-operative partner and will show the way, sometimes introducing you to a range of ideas and experiences that are quite freeing. There will be arguments – often – but they may be generated by you more than your **9**, who will simply retreat if the going gets too hard. Make sure you say what you really mean, and don't just speak for dramatic effect, for you will hurt **9**, who is deeply touched by many things humans suffer.

9 knows everyone, wants to travel everywhere, is interested in everything, artistically and literally. You may struggle to fit in all the interests you are drawn to, but will almost certainly push yourselves to be successful – and not just materially. **9** is more concerned with the things in life that touch the imagination or provoke serious thought, and this discipline is good for you. If anyone can convince you to take your skills that bit further, **9** will do so.

Be alert to **9**'s wounds from past affairs and childhood; **9**s always seem to be forced to cope with emotional experience in life, and sometimes conceal what has hurt them. If you – with your carping humour – try to take the lid off this potential Pandora's box, you may be unleashing more than you bargained for. Give **9** a little free time to party with other friends on occasion. Your largesse will be repaid.

Key themes

3 can turn **9**'s gloom into renewed hope, and respects **9**'s intelligence and depth · Co-operative partnership with much idealism · **9** inspires **3**'s best creative ideas and helps focus **3**'s energy

| 2 | 1 | 9 | 8 | 7 | 6 | 5 | 4 | 3 |

3 in love with an 11   ★★

When a **3** is involved with a **2** who is an **11**, this can be exhausting – like watching a pair of celebrities trying to outdo one another. You both have charisma and a vibrant character, but **3** may not trust **11** to be telling the whole truth and nothing but, and **11** feels **3** is sometimes guilty of being too flippant and superficial. What a shame you can't both join the same team and simply shine forth in the world! But the trouble is, these numbers are probably more likely to be competitive, and to undo each other's star qualities.

Oh yes! – you two are certainly drawn to each other. This has all the hallmarks of being a relationship of golden gods, that seemingly perfect pair who have it all. **3** is funny and attractive, and a party animal; **11** is multi-talented, extremely clever and above the average in virtually everything. Except humility? And is that why you find that the initial gloss between the two of you fades? It could be that neither of you can go on sharing the limelight, or making allowances for the other's ego all the time. Or it may be that you are both so busy making something of your lives in a public sphere that you have no real time to understand each other's needs, qualms, demons. **11** and **3** are likely to fall for appearances in one another, and be surprised on discovering that each has vulnerabilities which need attention.

In that very rare case that both of you are enlightened human beings right from an early age, and have learned to grow and become wiser from the undoubtedly extraordinary experiences of your lives (for no other number packs more into life than a **3** except, perhaps, an **11**!), then you may well be able to work at the highest level together – in which case, your bond may be exquisite. **11** illuminates the world for others, and makes you aware of the essential importance of your role in helping those who are hurt or have lost their way to laugh a little and find it again. 11, if mature, takes you by the hand and celebrates your vivid nature – your colour and energy, and your vitality.

But 11s take time to grow into their very big shoes, and in relationships they can be frustrating. And 3 – let's face it – is not a number renowned for its patience in letting others get on with their own dreams. Lovely, charming, gracious 3 wants a playmate to get drunk with – if need be – and put the world to rights through friendship. 11, in 3's mind, is on another planet ... and this is, perhaps, true in some ways.

Have a fling! Share each other's auras and keep each other busy for as long as it is a pleasure and there is no clash of egos. But don't rush to make long-term plans unless you are getting a little older and wiser and have learned to appreciate that everything in life demands some personal adjustment. **11** appeals to something in you, definitely, but the road is more than bumpy – it may be completely unpaved!

Key themes

Initial sense of daring and heightened awareness may pall to become a clash of egos and collision course of wills and desires • Magnetic attraction, but possibly short-lived

2   1   9   8   7   6   5   4   3

3 in love with a 22   ★★★

Just as with an **11**, a **4** born on the 22nd attracts you with their stand-out status and personal charm and charisma. But once the early attraction begins to fade, there may be trouble ahead ...

22 exudes authority, and may be authoritarian towards **3**, who is, after all, wanting to flit through life without too many heavy ties or demands. Certainly you are loyal and loving and affectionate, but **22** may seem too grown up for you – someone who was almost middle-aged in childhood. You see **22**'s powerful hold on others, the respect they command, the direction they want to take, the sobriety of their morals and expectations of others. And it doesn't seem to be for you.

And **22** might seek to change you. Though attracted to your humour and grace, your artistic ability, your sunny

3   4   5   6   7   8   9   1   2

optimism about the world and everyone in it, **22** expects everyone to know where they're going, what they want, how to get there. It is a patient number, but that in essence curtails **3**'s meandering spirit – the one that demands that life is to be experienced and *then* quantified. **22** may just seem too serious.

Unless you share another number in common (check your LIFE numbers; *see page 214*), or you have both been through enough private pain and quiet reflection to see that, in each other, you have all that is missing personally, this pairing could be tricky in terms of forming a lasting relationship. A truly enlightened **22** will see that your humour and sunshine, and your lightness of touch, is exactly what they need to borrow at times; and, in return, a solid **22**, with exceptional vision and a mind turned on higher human needs and characteristics, can help you to differentiate between what is really frivolous and what is important.

2   1   9   8   7   6   5   4   3

22 unquestionably loves deeply, and may make you feel beloved in a way you never imagined could be possible. And you may make **22** relax and loosen up — and actually agree that it is fair to have some pleasure in life. Then, the buzz you generate together may mature into powerful electricity which lights a path for many more people than just yourselves.

If you can be flexible enough to cope with **22**'s stubbornness, and if **22** can be calm enough to be unaffected by your thrashings, then the world around you will become a remarkable place to be in. And this is not out of the question, but it does depend on some aspects of mutuality and selflessness that are not especially common to the average human being. If you have found this — and each other — you are very lucky, and headed somewhere truly unique.

Key themes

Both see the world very differently, but have social roles
to fulfil • **3** makes **22** feel young and possibly more joyful,
and **22** is very solid for **3** to cling to • A marriage of
opposites, where success depends on other factors

Work

YOUR **WORK** COMPATIBILITY CHART

	1	2	3	4	5
With a 1	★★★★	★★★★★	★	★★★	★★★
With a 2	★★★★★	★★★	★★★	★★★★	★
With a 3	★	★★★	★★★★	★★	★★★★★
With a 4	★★★	★★★★	★★	★★★★★	★★★
With a 5	★★★	★	★★★★★	★★★	★★
With a 6	★★	★★★★★	★★★★	★★★★	★★★★
With a 7	★★★★★	★★★	★★★	★★★★★	★★
With an 8	★★★★★	★★★★★	★★★★★	★★★	★★★★
With a 9	★★★★	★★★	★★★★★	★★	★★★
With an 11	★★	★★★★	★★★	★★★★★	★★
With a 22	★★★★★	★★	★★★	★★★	★★★★

3   4   5   6   7   8   9   1   2

6	7	8	9	11	22
★★	★★★★★	★★★★★	★★★★	★★	★★★★★
★★★★★	★★★	★★★★★	★★★	★★★★	★★
★★★★	★★★	★★★★★	★★★★★	★★★	★★★
★★★★	★★★★★	★★★	★★	★★★★★	★★★
★★★★	★★	★★★★	★★★	★★	★★★★
★★★	★	★★★★	★★★	★★★★★	★★★★
★	★★★★	★★★	★★	★★★★	★★★★★
★★★★	★★★	★★★	★★★★	★★★★★	★★★★
★★★	★★	★★★★	★★★	★★★★★	★★★★★
★★★★★	★★★★	★★★★★	★★★★★	★★★★	★★★★★
★★★★	★★★★★	★★★★	★★★★★	★★★★★	★★★

2	1	9	8	7	6	5	4	3

3 working with a 1   ★

1 likes your creativity, but not your lack of organization. If left to a **3**, no decision would be reached, which is the opposite to what **1** wants (and quickly!). It could be argued that **1** has the willpower to help you settle on one front, but at work this is a poor formula for success. You, meanwhile, get on with everyone, and it chafes with **1** that even the tea break turns into a party around you. You always make time to listen to someone's tale – to **1**'s disapproval!

You're neither lazy nor unwilling to do a job. On the contrary, you put your hand to many things, being creative and amenable in all of them; and you are prepared to stay back, to be flexible about what you're asked. But **1** would be happier knowing an expert is in charge of any post. Something about your multi-faceted ability, or sometimes dilettantism, drives **1** to despair. You are each artistic, have

| 3 | 4 | 5 | 6 | 7 | 8 | 9 | 1 | 2 |

flair, exude energy, wit and charm, but you often transmit nervous energy, which makes **1** nervous; and you're not keen on **1**'s apparent tactlessness. **1** speaks too directly, to your taste, if something needs articulating, making you shiver when they are sometimes brutal to weaker people. Then again, you often weave circles just to make a difficult point. You each have different methods – even if you ultimately come to the same conclusion. You are genuinely talented, and have a way with things – it's just not **1**'s way.

On a good day, you will amuse a **1** and make them laugh when deadlines are too close or pressures mount. But, in other respects, you are two talented souls who brush each other up the wrong way; if you are working together, put some space between you and mind your tongues!

Key themes
Unpredictable · Volatile · Disorganized · Baffling but creative

2 · 1 · 9 · 8 · 7 · 6 · 5 · 4 · 3

3 working with a 2   ★★★

2 likes your creativity but is driven mad by your unusual organization. Both of you find it hard to push for a clear decision, and **2** will be irritated when you introduce yet another set of options. You do things so differently from **2**, who has unfair doubts about your concentration and commitment; but there are positives. **3** recognizes **2**'s ability to work behind the scenes with difficult customers, and, as **3** is such a good upfront person, this could be workable if you are given different arenas to move about in.

3 seems alarmingly flash to **2**, who prefers to be quiet and subtle, while **2** seems too cautious for **3**, who always likes to take chances in business – and usually pulls them off. **2** will be annoyed by your manner of chatting and being informal with everyone, and you will be frustrated when **2** pours water on your unusual but brilliant ideas.

3	4	5	6	7	8	9	1	2

But, given that **2** is so willing to be amicable, this work team can achieve a great deal if you just agree to do things differently and get on with it. You appreciate **2**'s negotiation skills, and value their more demure style of aesthetic input. You have the pizzazz, but **2** the taste – and, married, this can be an interesting cross-pollination.

Some days, you will amuse **2** and make them laugh just when they need it – when deadlines are too close, or personal pressures are at a peak. This is your gift for **2**. And **2** slows your racing pulse when you get a little too excitable. Just remember to accept that this is a swing, up one day, down the next, and to be your most tolerant selves when things get too bogged down.

Key themes
Creative • Good with people • Indecisive • Different working techniques

| 2 | 1 | 9 | 8 | 7 | 6 | 5 | 4 | 3 |

3 working with a 3   ★★★★

Clients here and there, multiple phone lines, desktop and laptop computers side by side: two **3**s working together are a hive of activity. And a lot of fun! You know how to keep each other's spirits up and make others envious of what you do – for it always looks like you're enjoying yourselves.

Communications, PR and the media are ideal fields: you have such a flair for charm and getting others to talk that this must form part of how you make a living. Working with another **3**, you can guess what's happening and rescue each other when you have to. And there's plenty of scope for you to switch roles when things reach boiling point. You will relish the varied tasks you give to each other, and your relationship will turn into a close friendship, too.

There could be difficulties when you are both pulling hard in opposite directions – which will happen sometimes,

3   4   5   6   7   8   9   1   2

as you keep so many balls in the air. And there may be tensions if you are both sharing the limelight, and things may become competitive. But, as a rule, you will find a way of balancing each other's energies, sheltering one another from too many outside demands. And the hospitality between you is first class, so that each week (or day!) ends in a good dinner out or lunch on the company. You find ways like this to cope with pressure and put stress in perspective.

Two **3**s together are ideally suited to run their own business: you can fill so many roles with flexibility and talent. Whatever you do, it will be something where others rely on you both for a rallying call to enjoy even the worst challenges. People gravitate to you in any grave situation!

Key themes

Fun alongside duty • Variety of work • Lucky with money • Socializing outside work

2   1   9   8   7   6   5   4   3

3 working with a 4   ★★

4 asks you to settle down to duty: not something you enjoy. This is like someone telling you to act your age, and you wonder why. But **4** wants you to focus on one thing and get it done before moving on to the next – and this is nearly impossible. Indeed, **3** is at its best juggling several things at once: this keeps you fresh and prevents you from lapsing into onerous duty and boredom. But **4** just doesn't grasp this, and feels you are freelancing, or moonlighting, or just avoiding responsibilities. It is difficult to communicate the truth without argument, and tempers may flare.

If you could put all this aside, and accept that you have markedly different styles at the office, you offer each other all that is missing from your individual portfolios. **4** has all the method you might well envy, and you all the social skill and verbal agility **4** would love to have. **4** is old-fashioned, while **3** likes to seek new ways to improve on worn-out techniques. This it shares with **1** and **5**, so if these numbers abound, poor **4** is apt to feel outnumbered – quite literally.

But **4** is essential somewhere in the organization for the smooth running of any business. **4** has such a practical mind, and is able to break down the most complicated project to make it fathomable for everyone. Without **4**, nothing can be accounted for properly, or delegated. You need **4**'s practical approach to make your ideas reach people. You'll simply have to find a way to give them their own domain, and keep to yours, because **4** will be driven mad by your chattering, charming, exuberant way of getting results. Chalk and cheese, perhaps – but there is room for both!

Key themes

Method versus madness • Sociability contrasted with taciturn concentration • Much tolerance needed!

2 1 9 8 7 6 5 4 3

3 working with a 5   ★★★★★

This is a coming together of the sports star and the photographer, or the actor and the talent agent – though which is which will occasionally be the question! You admire 5's drive and physical energy; plus, they really understand what you're on about when you go off on a flight of fancy. 5 promotes 3's ideas better than anybody, and 3 puts a frame around 5's cinematic visions. Together you achieve symmetry, your concepts overlapping well and your imagination bolstering each other. Both numbers are excellent at managing and inspiring people, and each has a feeling for the balance between what is necessary and what is enjoyable. You are, as it were, speaking the same language.

In any given sphere, and on any particular day, 5 may be 3's boss and 3 may be 5's; this is because you direct each other alternately. It may be hard to say who is more responsible for the other's success. Did **3** provide the perfect vehicle for **5**'s promotional skills? Or did **5** see a way to capitalize on **3**'s creative talents? Can **5** do without **3**'s imagination? No more than **3** could flourish without **5**'s support. In every way, you two attack things with gusto. Nothing is impossible, and you never give up or say die.

5's interests are likely to move **3**'s into new territories, too, and being around both of you will be a funny and pleasurable experience for your team-mates. If there's a **4** anywhere in the grouping, they may feel left behind once you two start on your run of ideas. One needs to be quick-witted to keep up. This is an occasionally competitive, but mostly highly entertaining, effective partnership.

Key themes
Both create buzz and a sense of what is possible •
Complementary skills and respect for each other's method

| 2 | 1 | 9 | 8 | 7 | 6 | 5 | 4 | 3 |

3 working with a 6 ★★★★

A strong understanding and sympathy helps the two of you find a way through all kinds of thorny problems. **6** is so visual and caring, and stands back applauding your talents for making everyone feel better after calamity. And no one gives more time to others than the two of you together – with **6** acting as healer or teacher, and you as entertainer and unpaid counsellor. You have a gift for bringing disparate people together and showing others how to get on to greater effect. Work-wise, this is a considerable skill.

You handle **6**'s serious nature without being disturbed by it, because you recognize that it's the product of caring and kindness to others. It is helpful in business, but liable to be oppressing if not alleviated by your buoyancy. **6** looks to you for guidance when efforts to avert personality clashes come to nothing. No one can lighten the atmosphere as well as you, and your willingness to turn your own hand to any task and make light of difficulties is inspirational to all. **6** appreciates your wisdom and sense of proportion.

You should be good at attracting money together, too, and will make the work environment feel beautiful. Both of you place an emphasis on the necessity of getting the aesthetic right – and, when it comes to dressing up for the job, you each have contrasting but admirable styles. You will truly respect each other. Don't let **6** unwittingly frighten you away from taking big, bold steps. **6** is more cautious than you, which sometimes has its place: but it is how you lend each other awareness of what is lacking that makes the work tie between you such a happy and productive one.

Key themes

Complementary relationship shows others how to achieve harmony • Both highly creative • Love of beautiful space

| 2 | 1 | 9 | 8 | 7 | 6 | 5 | 4 | 3 |

3 working with a 7   ★★★

When you give each other room to function smoothly, this work relationship may be better than its three-star rating might suggest. **3** can appreciate **7**'s skills and ability to specialize in one field, knowing everything about it. This is not the way you do things, but you recognize that somebody should. What will bother you is if **7** seems a little arrogant or high-handed about their own contributions.

In fact, **7** can frustrate you at work, because their very clever humour is often biting and negative, and their tongue often critical and shrewd. You would rather find a solution to personnel problems than simply identify them, and you may feel that **7** is caught up in their own space, own world, own interests. It is true that a **7** in the office can seem selfish – but if you gently bring this to their attention, they are astonishingly gracious and willing to modify their direction. **7** may be blinkered, but is neither cruel nor unconcerned with other people's needs.

3's talent is to dip and dive and hustle – which **7** can appreciate, but wouldn't want to replicate. This is a work tie that demands – and usually achieves – mutual respect and a little room for manoeuvre. **7** is best left to get on with things, and you may not always understand how or why they do things as they do; but you will, nevertheless, trust their intentions and appreciate the results they get. Just make sure you don't use their personal coffee mug without thinking!

Key themes

Different approaches (flamboyant/dignified) bring interesting results • Respect for each other essential

2   1   9   8   7   6   5   4   3

3 working with an 8   ★★★★★

A shared sense of purpose brings you two together for a really first-rate business bond. 8 understands how you think and why you do what you do – and really appreciates your tact and style. You can charm any reluctant client or third party into agreement – at any price, it seems – and 8 uses your people skills as the jumping-off point for their own designs in business. No one has a better head for what has real potential than an 8, and you will give everything to help them get the desired end result.

8 trusts 3 to come up with those appealing little twists and necessary variations on a theme which make for a more harmonious work environment. Knowing you have the humour to cope with any emergency, you may be asked to take on a pressure situation by 8, where other numbers fail to see you have what it takes. 8 is completely

at ease with your facile mind, good memory and witty way of deflecting criticism or crisis. In short, nobody gives you more leeway to shine, or more benefit of the doubt about your imaginative propositions. **5** takes you as fun, **3** as a kindred spirit ... but **8** takes you seriously.

And who else besides a **3** recognizes the intentions of the **8**'s brilliance? Others may think **8** is being too clever for the world, but if there is any way of popularizing their genius **3** will find that way. And, together, you will bring a whirr of activity and a sense of pride in achievement to everyone working with you. **3** nurses **8** through many sleepless nights – and into a sunny new day!

Key themes

3 recognizes **8**'s professionalism, and **8** happily gives **3** opportunity • Bounce off one another's energies and visions • Very good prospects for success

2   1   9   8   7   6   5   4

3 working with a 9   ★★★★

This is another potentially good working partnership, as you both know how to work hard when the mood takes you and when you are feeling motivated. **9** has almost as vivid an imagination as you do, and together you find many ways to repackage old ideas and make them more modern and relevant. **9** has moral integrity, too, which you will find refreshing, as you often feel that subordinates are given either unfair treatment or not enough credit for what they do. Under the direction of a **9**, life is kinder for everyone.

Moreover, a **3** can always out-talk a **9** (not usually easy!), and win a point for other people who have something to say. **9** will listen to you and do you the courtesy of heeding your advice, knowing it is based on sharp instinct. You also have a way of making the sometimes over-serious **9** see the funny side of a situation. Together, you will disarm your adversaries or competition, and walk away with the prize everyone was seeking!

Go into the travel, theatrical, publishing or even underwear business together: you have the facility of recognizing where the world is going and what it needs to entertain and equip it on the way. You both genuinely like people, and this means you can feel your time is well spent on any outlet which caters for people. This is distinctly different from the mindset of a **7**, perhaps, or a **1**, both of whom like to work in isolation, and who get it right – where the public's taste is concerned – almost as a matter of mediation. You and **9** know, upfront and personal, how people feel. You feel it with them.

Key themes
Understand the public's taste • Work in tandem • Good humour and amenable relationships with others

2   1   9   8   7   6   5   4   3

3 working with an 11   ★★★

Not quite the same as with a **2**, you work in a different way with an **11**. What is often testing on a personal level can be endured for a reason at work. **11** has a rather fragile ego but a very good mind for the unusual, and an understanding of how people tick deep inside. This marries with your instinct, and your skill for reading others from their body language, so that, together, you have a way of picking up on exactly what is needed in any one project or in a business plan. **11** spots this, and turns to you for ideas on how to disarm any combative voices. And, moody as **11** can be, you admire their strength and talent, and sheer force of will. **11** often sets you a banner to follow, and you have the energy to take things up to the next level.

Personal differences set aside, you may find that an **11** is truly inspirational at work. Mood swings are a problem for each of you, and the **11** may become very down and contemplative in all the worst ways if there are personal dramas happening at home. This makes the dips and swings in your energy seem like child's play. You also have to help an **11** to see that every challenge is just another opportunity for excellence. There is almost something of an obsessive/compulsive nature about an **11**, but **3** has the power to rally their spirits, and have them scaling the battlements more determinedly than ever before.

And this is your role, because if you marry your charm to **11**'s, your instinct to their telepathic intensity, your vision to their brilliance, the world may be the better for it. Try to put egos aside.

Key themes

Almost psychic ability to read people · Ahead of the crowd in identifying future business direction

| 2 | 1 | 9 | 8 | 7 | 6 | 5 | 4 | 3 |

3 working with a 22   ★★★

Teamwork between these numbers can be rewarding, but there is a tendency at work for one or the other to take the lead, depending on requirement – and **22** is never used to someone else in charge. Not to speak unfairly, anyone born on the 22nd has a patience and aptitude for hard work and concentration that can be an asset to a **3**, when they are skipping from one duty to another. However, **22** likes things done quietly and without a fanfare, while **3** loves to release its tensions through talk and expressed emotions. Your different approaches – not just to work, but to life – can take some adjustments on both sides.

You are often seen as the party boy or girl – the big noise, with charm and too many talents to make sense of – while **22**, so steady, reliable and mature, tends to be unfairly viewed as sober and uninteresting. There is, in fact,

| 3 | 4 | 5 | 6 | 7 | 8 | 9 | 1 | 2 |

almost nothing a **22** can't do to contribute to the smooth running of a business or corporation, but they have their own ideas about where their energies are best spent. And this doesn't always make sense to a **3**, who is garrulous and explosive and witty, and lives for the moment. Yet, when you need to rely on someone else's judgement, you will look up to a **22**!

Give each other some room, time and scope to tackle things in contrasting styles. Try not to deprecate **22**'s inherent superiority and sense system, and ask that they extend you the same courtesy, and appreciate that you can have a serious side and be very deep too. Then, miracles may happen, and a mutual-admiration society be founded!

Key themes

PhD versus Oscar-winning actor • Bring different strengths to a task • Achieve greatness together

2 1 9 8 7 6 5 4 **3**

Friendship

YOUR **FRIENDSHIP** COMPATIBILITY CHART

	1	2	3	4	5
With a 1	★★★	★★★★★	★★	★★★	★★★
With a 2	★★★★★	★★	★★★	★★★★	★
With a 3	★★	★★★	★★★★	★	★★★★
With a 4	★★★	★★★★	★	★★★★★	★★
With a 5	★★★	★	★★★★	★★	★★★
With a 6	★	★★★★	★★★★★	★★★	★★★★
With a 7	★★★★	★★★★★	★★★★	★★★★★	★
With an 8	★★★★	★★★★	★★★★★	★★	★★★★
With a 9	★★★★	★★★	★★★★	★★★★	★★★★
With an 11	★★★	★★★★★	★★	★★★★★	★★
With a 22	★★★	★★★	★★★★	★★	★★★

3	4	5	6	7	8	9	1	2

6	7	8	9	11	22
★	★★★★	★★★★	★★★★	★★★	★★★
★★★★	★★★★★	★★★★	★★★	★★★★★	★★★
★★★★★	★★★★	★★★★★	★★★★	★★	★★★★
★★★	★★★★★	★★	★★★★	★★★★★	★★
★★★★	★	★★★★	★★★★	★★	★★★
★★★★	★	★★★★	★★★★	★★★	★★★★★
★	★★★★	★★★	★★	★★★★★	★★★★★
★★★★	★★★	★★★★	★★★★	★★★★★	★★★
★★★★	★★	★★★★	★★	★★★★	★★★★
★★★	★★★★★	★★★★★	★★★★	★★★★★	★★★★
★★★★★	★★★★★	★★★	★★★★	★★★★	★★

2	1	9	8	7	6	5	4	3

The life and soul of any party, you get on with virtually everyone, though some individuals will test your charm and humour! Let's see which are the best combinations ... and which are the worst:

3 and 1 (★★): A little too much conflict over the basic necessities of life. **1** is worn out by **3**'s fragmented energy, and **3** doesn't like the way **1** assumes natural priority, though does recognize their flair. Egos are the big difficulty here – for both of you.

3 and 2 (★★★): Like you, **2** is kind and sociable, but your style may seem too noisy for them! **3**'s efforts to make others laugh when they are low will bring a censorious reaction from **2**, who favours a gentler approach. Also, **2** thinks **3** fickle about their love life. Friends, yes, but not too close.

3 and **3** (★★★★): Good company is on offer with some-one who shares your number. You are energetic and amused by the same things, ready to listen to each other, enjoy one another's way of seeing and mimicking the passing world. A long-term friendship.

3 and **4** (★): This will test your charms! You cope well with a **4** in the office if you respect the work they do, but as friends you have very different values. **4** is rarely impressed with your instinctive way of seducing others socially, and trust may be minimal.

3 and **5** (★★★★): Instantly drawn to each other, you see through **5**'s vulnerabilities and their efforts to offset them, and **5** has this skill with you. Good drinking pals, you also know you are both wiser and more serious, on occasion, than the rest of the world sees.

2   1   9   8   7   6   5   4   3

3 and **6** (★★★★★): You love your **6** friends, and will keep them and grow with them for years. They appreciate your warmth, as well as your sense of fun and resilience to depression. **6** recognizes your true talents and the cast of your mind. A natural friendship.

3 and **7** (★★★★): Not great lovers, you two get on well without romantic complications. You challenge and provoke one another in quite positive ways. You may allow a **7** to tell you when you are being giddy, and they listen when you point out that they are wallowing over some issue. Honesty is strong between you.

3 and **8** (★★★★★): This relationship is good on every front — love, work and friendship. There is a shared judgement and respect between you. **8** makes you more serious in a good way, and you make **8** laugh and express their own gallows humour at crucial times. Lifelong friendship.

| 3 | 4 | 5 | 6 | 7 | 8 | 9 | 1 | 2 |

3 and **9** (★★★★): Also a good friendship. **9** is a social bunny – though perhaps more generally and less intimately with others than you. You articulate the emotions **9** is feeling so well that there may be true confidences shared between you. **9** is your 'elder sibling'.

3 and **11** (★★): Have a passionate fling with an **11**, but don't ask them to be your best friend. **11**s are on another planet, as far as you can see, and there is likely to be no lack of subject matter for conversation, but also argument. Stimulating, I suppose!

3 and **22** (★★★★): Friendship works, where love or business may not. The different styles, yet sincere respect you have for each other, offers good company when you need it. **22** is a profound adviser, and you can unbutton them more than most. You love **22**'s cleverness, and you lead each other to new discoveries. Just don't live together!

3 IN OTHER PLACES

So what does it mean when your number turns up on a house? Do you live in a 3 home? And how does the number 3 affect your pet – or even the car that you drive? Numbers exude a subtle influence on everything in our lives; and here are just a few examples of how ...

3 4 5 6 7 8 9 1 2

A 3 address

If the number of your address – or of your apartment – reduces back to a **3**, just try keeping people away! They will drop in and bring a bottle, expect you to have a cake ready for tea and a chat, or just pop in for some company and conversation. It is a natural hive of activity, upbeat, probably pretty, and lucky financially, too – perfect if you have to turn your home into an office!

If this is your love nest, don't be surprised if there is often a 'third person' to take into the equation. Is there an ex? A baby on the way? A family member who always wants to be there? Or maybe your partner has a close friend who loves your couch? Not the perfect address for a couple on honeymoon, maybe, but in every other way a **3** home is a pleasure to inhabit. Just don't expect too much privacy if you live there.

A 3 pet

If you don't know your pet's birthday, use the first letter of their name to calculate their number. If it's a C, L or U, they're a **3**. The **3** pet is a playful animal who is entertaining to everyone. Not a companion to bark at the postman or alert you to an intruder in any disapproving way, this pet likes company, and loves to be stroked and admired. Watch that eyebrow shoot upward when you talk about them, and just see how your **3** dog or cat preens and stretches when a possible playfellow arrives for a coffee. There are times when you may feel upstaged by a four-legged **3**!

This is not a pet to spend the day snoozing – although they can certainly be something of a dreamer. In the main, this theatrical creature wants to accompany you on your rounds – shopping, visiting, walking – even if it's a cat or rabbit! This is a brilliant number if you want your animal family member to be a true friend.

3   4   5   6   7   8   9   1   2

A 3 car

If the numbers of your licence plate reduce to **3**, your car must belong, somehow, in the limelight. Exciting, a good road performer, and bound to attract admiring glances from those you pass ... it's impossible to imagine an old-fashioned or practical car bearing this number.

It has a quirky personality, and may become part of your own image, for **3** is accessory-conscious and has a charm beyond its obvious attributes. Whether this car is expensive or a bargain-hunter's delight, it has panache and seems to say you are witty and good company. And, although it has moody-wet-morning days as well as immediate-start-up ones, it is *always* stylish.

YOUR LIFE NUMBER
Your lesson to learn

The time has come to consider the other main number in your numerology chart: your Life Lesson, or LIFE, number. This is sometimes also called the 'Birth Force'. Just as for the DAY number, calculating your LIFE number is easy: simply add together each digit of your full birth date (day, month and year), and keep adding the digits until they reduce to a single number (*see example on page 270*).

And that's it. You have your Life number. So what does it tell us?

3   4   5   6   7   8   9   1   2

What does it mean?

The **LIFE** number takes times to show its mark. You should see its influence over many years, and understand that it is representative of certain strengths and weaknesses that we learn to live with through years of experience. These characteristics need to be analysed over time, and it can take a while for us to come to know ourselves truly from our **LIFE** number. Uncovering these aspects of our character is a process of discovery, and we often don't fully recognize the traits of this number as clearly, or as quickly, as those of the stronger **DAY** number.

Once you have done your sums and discovered this second important number, you'll want to find out what this means. If your **LIFE** and **DAY** numbers are the same, this powerfully reinforces the qualities of your own number, and accentuates both strengths and weaknesses. You won't be fighting corners within your personality by having

2   1   9   8   7   6   5   4   3

two numbers to live with that are, perhaps, miles apart in spirit. But then, equally, if your numbers are the same you may lack a broad vision of the world, seeing with very sharp eyes through just a single (though enormous!) window.

On the following pages we will examine what your **DAY** number **3** is like in tandem with each other number, beginning with the powerful doubling of **3 DAY** and **3 LIFE**, and then moving on through all other possible combinations. If you discover you have a **LIFE** number which totals **11** or **22**, before it reduces to a final single digit of **2** or **4**, read the entry for **3** and **2**, or **3** and **4**, but also pay special attention to any extra information given relating to the added significance of the number being a variation of a master number.

SAME **DAY** AND **LIFE** NUMBER

As a double 3, you could well experience twice the fun of your number! Double the entertainment value, double the capacity to amuse the world. Your witty one-liners would be a hot property for any advertising agency or comedy act. You can be cynical, but generally your remarks are intended – and taken – in such good tenor by others that you give little offence. Like Jane Austen's Elizabeth Bennet, no matter how incisive you are, you say everything with a mixture of such archness and sweetness that you acquire many friends.

2   1   9   8   7   6   5   4   3

Two **3**s together make it easy for you to acquire such worldly success and luck that many will envy you. You will gain numerous possessions, but will also set these aside, thirsting for something more. The double dose of **3** often contributes to a greater sense of spirituality, and you have very high ideals. You may be the most romantic of all the **3**s, and you appreciate beauty and the arts above all. Your artistic ability is pronounced, in fact, and, even if you don't paint, sculpt or write yourself, you will appreciate the work of others, and have an excellent critical factor for what is good.

You are affectionate and loyal, though still a social butterfly, and flattery and deception have little place in your make-up. You conduct yourself with truth and fairness, and to your friends and partner you are faithful and trustworthy, and valued for your moral integrity. Many appreciate your good advice about business and affairs of the heart, and you are especially charitable and generous.

It's true to say that if you could fix the woes of the world you happily would do so.

Double trouble?

Yes, you have your downside. You are reluctant, perhaps, to assume responsibility, and this is partly because you fear personal failure. For this reason you may become dependent on others, or allow your talents to lay dormant. It is even possible that the **3** number-tendency for indecisiveness could be your complete undoing.

But this is only on your worst days, for, in fairness, there is a strong practical side to your nature, and you harness your gifts to achieve definite results. You will charm the builder into giving you the best job for a little less money, and convince your boss that you are irreplaceable and yet still get them to agree to give you a day off on more-than-regular occasions. You are elastic about these rules but not a cheat, for you have true nobility in your character.

The stand-out feature of your personality is that you love life, and, as long as life has been fair to you in your early years, you are a radiant and giving person. You really enjoy bringing pleasure to others – creating surprises, dropping by unexpectedly, turning up when you are most needed as if by magic. You are very magnetic, and will have many admirers. Expressive and blessed with the art of conversation, you love to live the good life. You do not seem to push yourself forwards, and yet you like to be on the stage and can be very entertainin. If you develop your ability to influence others, this will become a very satisfying vocational direction.

Lucky blessing

Foibles? You prefer to wear nice clothes, and like to show off the label just for confidence; and you definitely like

| 3 | 4 | 5 | 6 | 7 | 8 | 9 | 1 | 2 |

to be appreciated. Sometimes you do everyday things in a grandiose way — too much eating or drinking, too spendthrift, very self-indulgent — and you may overreact, making mountains out of molehills. Are you a gossip? You are certainly generous enough to admit this if it's the case, but do try to avoid the temptation to live just for the moment.

The positive pleasure of being both **DAY** and **LIFE** number **3** is that you will be lucky in most of your day-to-day occurrences — finding just the right house at the price you can afford, just the right lover in the place you want to be, and just the right framework for business. Travel is certain to come your way, not because it's associated with your number so much as because you attract variety and movement and activity like a magnet. You need, and will draw to you, a constantly changing run of experiences and events, and you will have friends — quite probably — in many parts of the country, or many corners of the world.

If you can minimize the urge to gamble — both literally and in life — you should be fortunate in general, since your luck is derived from your optimistic outlook on life. People flock to help you, and you reciprocate in kind. This is truly a pair of numbers to regard as a blessing.

DIFFERENT **DAY** AND **LIFE** NUMBERS

Most of us will find that we have two different birthday numbers, and this can be an advantage. One number may soften the single track of the other, and mean we can see other people's viewpoints more easily. At other times, though, the numbers may be in real conflict – and this leads to vacillation in our reactions to everyday situations, or confusion about why we want to run one way and then another.

In the following pages you will discover how your own two numbers are likely to work together, and what you can do to maximize the potential of both when they are paired up.

2   1   9   8   7   6   5   4   3

3 Day with 1 Life

These two numbers are sometimes at loggerheads when they meet as two individuals, but operating within one personality they usually find much better expression. The effect of **1** and **3** is to heighten the creativity of your **DAY** number and make you very driven to produce artistic perfection. Both numbers are energetic, and the **1**'s single-mindedness dominates the **3**'s distressing indecisiveness: you will get things done! **3** also adds an emotional power, which helps push you to do things that matter even more to your sense of fair play.

Sometimes the **1** pulls the **3 DAY** number into even greater extravagance than usual, for **1** can show off a little and be impulsive. But a happier outcome is that the **3** adds to **1**'s ambition and dynamism a gift for talking or writing, and a true talent shines out. With the support of your **3**

DAY number, the often lonely **1** will learn over the years how to talk to people, so that you don't retire into your own shell when you are hurt. **1** draws on **3**'s happiness and optimism, and allows you to mix with a wider group of people than **1** often chooses to do. Equally, the scattered energies one associates with **3** are refined through **1**'s determination, so that the self-expression of both numbers is at a peak.

The one danger of having **3 DAY** and **1 LIFE** numbers joined together is that your excellent ideas get lost in too much talk. **3** is a chatterer, and given to some degree of exaggeration, while **1** likes the sound of its own voice, at times, and can be boastful. If these traits exacerbate each other, there is a wastefulness and a chance of giving in to delusions of grandeur which eclipses the inspirational strengths of both numbers, normally so positive. There is also a possibility that both numbers lapse from genuine innovation to faddishness, and fail to produce anything outstanding. Generally, though, the artistic drive of these two numbers is sufficient to help you work well with your talents and achieve a great deal over your lifetime, and the warm-heartedness of **3** will steer **1** away from its potential to loneliness.

If anyone offends you, you may be especially unforgiving, for **3** hates to have its kind nature thrown in its face. Perceptiveness should help you avoid this, though, and if you are quick to anger you are just as quick to move on. Always make sure there are elements of creativeness in your work or your leisure hours, for without this you may feel as though you have been denied something important in your life.

3 Day with 2 Life

Again, here are two numbers that can be at loggerheads when they meet as individuals, but which tend to find much better expression when operating within one personality. **2** has the kind of good taste and quiet dignity that lends gravity to **3**, which can often be boisterous on its own; and **3** gives **2** a little more pluck, and courage to stand up and say what it wants. Both numbers are popular in different spheres, so the effect of both together is to make a personality with radiance, energy *and* serenity when it matters. Quite a package!

  3 pulls **2** through the hedge when it feels like retiring, and adds vigour to the spiritual qualities of the **2**. And if the **2** is actually **11**, this will feel even more the case, for **3** really is like a pep pill that fuels **11**'s physical stamina and helps to make a business or an achievement out of what may be just an inspired spiritual dream. And then, too, **3** is aided by **2** being more still and, sometimes, quiet in terms of thinking, so that the impact of both numbers together is of a beautiful and harmonious flower garden organized in a symphony of whites and creams of perfect height and shape – now and then made dramatic with a splash of colour. The mental energies, people skills, speaking ability, creative flair – all gain an infusion of colour from the existence of **3** with the number **2**.

The one potential glitch with a **3** DAY and a **2** LIFE number coming together is that **2**'s wonderful organizational ideas can get a bit lost behind too much talk or too many possibilities. **3** is a chatterer and an entertainer, given to some degree of exaggeration, while **2** needs calm to tackle so many tasks in both the private and the career domain. Having such a predominant **3** can make **2** lose its certainty and direction. On the whole, though, the numbers complement each other, and make **2** more resilient and

| 3 | 4 | 5 | 6 | 7 | 8 | 9 | 1 | 2 |

less affected by the moods or imagined slights of others. Thus, in life generally, the two numbers emit positivity and charm to such a degree that you are likely to be spoiled for choice with friends, business associates and – yes – lovers too! ... And so the indecision that is latent in **2** but prevalent in **3** really comes to the fore. But how funny you are to listen to, talking about it!

The talents of both numbers are predominantly creative, so a likely career direction is in the area of the arts or working with people in publicity or public relations. Fashion will be interesting for you too, and the **3** draws out **2**'s ability to entertain in many spheres. But don't be surprised if deciding where to place all your energies is not so straightforward, and choice – once again – becomes almost a bane!

3 Day with 4 Life

You are a drama queen, even though your **4 LIFE** number tries to disguise this. Although **4** adds concentration and application to zany **3**, **3** always offsets **4**'s practicality with a flair for making a life full of incidents. True, having the **4** gives you the strength to stick at tasks and to transform your work and plans into some kind of reality, but your creative imagination and enthusiasm for ideas which leave others bewildered is what earmarks you.

Your **3 DAY** number bestows the ability to express your experience of life with gritty humour, and you encapsulate the essence of people and events with colourful phrases, but **4** makes you sit back a little, and stops you from saying inappropriate things *most* of the time. You prefer it when people come to you, and, 'Godfatheresque', you never do the apologizing. **4** undermines **3**'s normal confi-

3   4   5   6   7   8   9   1   2

dence with a little insecurity — not always a bad thing — and your need to feel loved means that the best of people always fall into your life.

Having **4** as the other dominant number in your life, you have a more practical ability to appraise people and situations for their true worth; and your concentration level is excellent. You understand the details behind every project — no bad thing for a **3** — and you accept that work and effort are required. **3** will always bestow humour, charm and a restless spirit, but **4** establishes that vital ingredient of 'method', so that you construct a tangible world in your fairy-tale imagination. Other **3**s build castles in the air, but your castles are real enough, and have central heating and luxurious bathrooms!

4s have ability in many creative areas, notably being able with your hands, but you may also have fancy footwork, and be a skilful dancer or sportsperson. In business you are also capable of helping others, for **4** is more patient than **3** – yet **3**, of course, blesses you with an approachable personality. **4** alters **3**'s sociability by making you more selective in your personal friendships and business associations; and, perhaps thankfully, it makes you more careful with your possessions, and a better manager of your daily life. **3** and **4** working together are also likely to accentuate the more reticent side of your character, highlighting **3**'s sensitivity and disinclination for criticism. However, backed up by **4**, you are more likely to shrug off rude comments, deciding that whoever bestowed it is beneath your attention.

The combination of talents from these numbers should make you very successful in dealing with property or houses, gardens, music and the entertainment industry. You will also have a unique personal taste in jewellery and accessories. Avoid any get-rich-quick schemes, but be sure **3** still bathes you in more than your share of luck. The presence of the **4** simply helps you to actualize your dreams.

| 3 | 4 | 5 | 6 | 7 | 8 | 9 | 1 | 2 |

3 Day with 5 Life

For most of us, the very idea of such a supply of energy bound up in one person would make us faint. You are the showbiz committee and the booked act all in one go! Will you ever delegate? The biggest danger from having these two birthday numbers is that you will wear yourself thin, burn the candle at both ends – or any other metaphor that conveys the sense of someone packing their life with ideas and activities from dawn till dusk, and from the cradle to the grave.

You are very independent and value your freedom, and you love to get out in the world and participate in the symphony that is life. Far from urging you to concentrate on one stream of activity, you are actually at your best when you have many irons in the fire. You are impatient, restless, energetic, and have a low boredom threshold, so anyone who shares your life should be ready for an amusement park permanently erected in the back garden!

You always keep things moving, and **3**'s gift of the gab is taken to full measure when married with **5**'s vivid ability to produce quotable aphorisms. You will never spend unnecessary time getting banal things done, and you will chafe at the bit if you are forced into routine situations, because your destiny is to be both progressive and versatile, and to go boldly where none have dreamed of going before. Sometimes this makes you foolhardy, but nine times out of ten you will achieve the impossible, and leave others open-mouthed in your wake.

A comfortable home for a **3/5** will have a telephone in every room, a high-speed internet connection and a television in the kitchen. In fact, there is probably a radio in your shower, for you are always listening to what others have to say, engaging in it, and disagreeing constantly. You have an inability to finish all of the many tasks that you have on the go, and your mind is always on the next job. For the most part, though, you exude such authority that other people become inveigled in your plans and find themselves carrying out the banalities for you. It is a talent, but one you will not always be admired for.

3 and **5** heighten each other's creative talents. It is almost inconceivable that, with these numbers, you would not paint, write, sing and/or dance, have an excellent eye for photography, and make anything that is normally routine much more unusual. **5** with **3** also brings out a talent for legal matters, civil service issues and any other facets of business that require a feeling for documentation. In short, this DAY/LIFE combination will make such a splash in this world that the rest of us should be sure to give you the whole pool.

2 1 9 8 7 6 5 4 3

3 Day with 6 Life

The most domestic variation for any number **3**, a **6 LIFE** number will help you concentrate your energies on creating a perfect home that is beautiful, functional, and a haven for everyone to visit. You will adore your children, and be permanently inspired with ways to create a feast for their senses — **6** prioritizing family, as it does, and **3** the best number at romping on the floor with toddlers to teens.

Your ability in the pure arts is pronounced, especially with a gift for design and fashion, but also with a strong taste for drama and music. You may prefer to work in an artistic field from home, if possible, but **3** saves **6** from its inclination to close off from the world at times. Though **6** is serene, **3** is vibrant, and a blending of these characteristics will set the style for your life pattern. Sometimes outgoing, sometimes introverted, you will surprise yourself with

| 3 | 4 | 5 | 6 | 7 | 8 | 9 | 1 | 2 |

your varying taste for whether to stay in or hit the town.

One of **6**'s failings is to be obstinate or overly traditional, but here **3** comes to the rescue, making you more
inclined to react to testing circumstances with some flexibility, and to try new things rather than retreat to the
familiar. Equally, **6** calms **3**, and allows you to feel that
time spent on recreation and relaxation is justified, especially if this means you can indulge your family in luxuri-
ant pursuits shared with them alone. You will undoubtedly
be a good cook, as happy catering a children's birthday
party or a picnic in the woods as tea with the vicar or a
visit from the in-laws. You can gauge the requirements of
any situation to the letter, and have an uncanny knack of
choosing exactly what is right for any occasion. And you
are renowned for your skill at choosing a perfect gift for
a quirky individual, or saying the right thing to a friend in a
crisis. Sensitivity combined with originality are the corner-
stones of your personality.

2   1   9   8   7   6   5   4   3

At some point in your life you may go through a crisis of identity, where you must decide how it is that you would like the world to see you. It will affect everything: your choice of career and selection of partner. Your sense of yourself is very important, and you don't like to be labelled by others. **6** is very sensitive to making a good impression and cares what the world thinks, while **3** needs to be seen as charming and a good person. If you feel you are being underestimated by anyone around you, it will create a deep wound. For this reason, take time and care about your educational choices and where you want to be in the world. You need to respect yourself, and, with this achieved, you will always draw gracious respect in turn from everyone around you.

3   4   5   6   7   8   9   1   2

3 Day with 7 Life

A life lesson of **7** adds some healthy sobriety to exuberant **3**, and makes you discerning and self-critical, though still very artistic and appreciative of people. Kind-hearted and a good judge of character, you will nevertheless withdraw into your shell more often than any other **3**. A relationship which gives you breathing space and time by yourself is a virtual must. Your taste is impeccable – the **7** accentuating this quality from **3** – and your memory rapier-sharp, though selective. You hang on to a kind deed or a cruel hurt in equal measure.

7 is the number of truth and, as **3** urges you to speak, you will have much of value to say. It is unusual for you to take anything at face value because you size up situations astutely, but your **DAY** number **3** helps you to exude such easy charm that others may be unaware that they are

2   1   9   8   7   6   5   4   3

being analysed. The numbers together give you powerful intuitive skills, and it is hard to imagine anyone pulling the wool over your eyes.

However, you can be surprisingly idealistic, and invest great expectation in those you love. A refined sensibility leads you to hope that everyone else will behave with moral goodness, and it will hurt when they inevitably let you down. Coping with these punches is something you will do after many years of gradually hardening yourself to some of life's realities.

But the entertainment committee has not deserted you just because of the presence of serious-thinking **7**. You plan out – and execute – star-studded events with exactitude. Full of resources, you know exactly where to find a stork ice sculpture for the baby shower, or a unicorn *piñata* for the church fete. You can find ice cream in the Amazon and a taxi at midnight on New Year's Eve; and if anyone can charm the parking attendant out of issuing a ticket on

Fifth Avenue, it will be you! The irresistible blend of **7**'s inner serenity and elegance with the charm and natural flirtatiousness of **3** is at its peak in this number-pairing.

You should work for yourself, for you are all things to all people. Independent as well as sociable, focused as well as multi-faceted, you manage to see a dozen tasks to their conclusion all at once. Like a Bach fugue, your character encompasses many themes working together with great complexity: lightness with gravity, friendliness with reticence. Allow yourself the scope to respond to circumstances in different ways on different days. And don't be worried if you constantly surprise even yourself.

3 Day with 8 Life

This combination of numbers could be anything from a hurricane to a gentle breeze, for both numbers have power and people skills. Whether they huff and puff and blow your house down, or simply act as a breath of fresh air, will depend largely on circumstances.

Charming in social situations, you could blag the crown jewels from a beefeater and still have time for tea – and my, don't you like to take tea in swish places! Your membership to the latest hip club is a requisite starting point, and when you join the school picnic you'll want to pack a hamper from an exclusive store and spread out a cashmere tartan rug. You will beat all the other parents in the family race just so you can say, 'I'm a terrible runner,' and woe betide someone who does not produce a formal apology for missing your birthday.

3   4   5   6   7   8   9   1   2

For here is a blending of appreciation for quality and a generous nature. You are loved by all who work with you, and are known as the life and soul of the party. Most competitive with yourself, you expect others to give their all on every occasion, and anything less than perfect is not to be accepted. Vivacious and enticing, you can also be bad-tempered and moody, and your partner will have to be a very patient person. **3** demands colour from life and **8** is a power number, with the consequent effect that even fun is a serious business. True, you have an innate sense of what will fire the imagination of the marketplace and, if you don't work in television or PR, your skills are wasted. Throwing yourself whole-heartedly into each venture, be it American quilting or redecorating a whole room to complement one piece of furniture, your aesthetic eye has extra vision.

Just remember that your personal drive and need for results can be a burden to others, as not everyone moves at your pace or dances to your tune. But if anyone needs a counsellor, or an ear, or a voice of quiet reason, yours is the one. You make light of what is heavy, and see a calm path across volcanic ground. The ease and charm with which you seemingly undertake each task is the envy of all around you, but be aware that not everyone has read the works of Shakespeare twice. Your passion for literature gives you a enquiring mind but can make you a tad snobby about those less well-educated than yourself. The two sides of the **8**'s character are accentuated by the juggling **3**, making you good at many things but difficult to please.

3 Day with 9 Life

3 seeks the limelight and **9** is the actor, so in some sense your life must be theatrical. You are a great raconteur and can enter into the spirit of other people's stories, dressing the funniest situations in elegant phrases, and laughing heartily at those personal dramas that test you often in your life, no matter how much the laughter belies the pain.

You are philanthropic with a kind outlook on your fellow beings, and, although you are not always able to live up to your personal expectations, you do have a philosophical way of handling disappointment. **9** added to **3** emphasizes your natural degree of compassion and generosity, and you are sympathetic and more selfless than **3** is often given credit for. Because **9** is the mirror number, you entice others to open up to you and show you their feelings, and are then able to surprise them by reflecting back just what it is that they've said. You are often able to illuminate aspects of people's characters in ways no one else manages. This talent alone would make you a good writer or dramatist.

By turns, you can be generous and tolerant or critical and demanding. You love to help others, but may be surprised when they put space between you and them, for fear of disappointing you. You don't mean to be bossy, but **9** naturally takes the lead – which is perhaps good for **3**, which sometimes thrashes about to no purpose. Both numbers are emotional, so you may love deeply and be hurt often. Your number **3** helps you to find your own destiny, although **9** has strong issues with the father figure: how will this manifest in your life? Maybe you will seek others whose authority you admire, or perhaps no one will ever live up to your own father; but you have the power to be a good surrogate parent to others, and a skill for seeing something lovely in what others may find almost ugly.

3   4   5   6   7   8   9   1   2

Both numbers give you a beauty and grace of character, and yet each number exacerbates some of the uncertainty of the other. Let others decide on the unimportant things in life — which restaurant to choose, or what colour for a cushion. You are bent on issues concerning what it seems *important* to achieve, and if you utilize your many talents you may be able to direct our attention to places where it is needed. This number-pairing has the power to show us the way.

THE FUTURE
Take a look what's in store...

And now we come to the calculation of your future. Each year, on your birthday, you move into a new sphere of number-influence which governs that year. The numbers progress in cycles of nine years; after nine years, the cycle starts over again, and a whole new period of your life begins afresh. The cycle can be applied to every number, so you can discover what the main issues will be for partners, friends and family, as well as for yourself, in any given year (*see calculation instructions, opposite*). Emphasis is placed on what will happen to you when you are in your own year number – that is, in any '**3**' year cycle.

| 3 | 4 | 5 | 6 | 7 | 8 | 9 | 1 | 2 |

Working out your cycle

To find out what year you're currently in, use the same formula employed for calculating the **LIFE** number, but substitute the current year for the year in which you were born. Every year, the cycle then moves on by one more number until, after a **9** year, returning to **1**, to begin the cycle again.

Calculation example 1

BIRTHDAY: 30 January 1971

TO CALCULATE THE CURRENT YEAR NUMBER: $3+0+1+\underbrace{\left[2+0+0+7\right]}_{\text{CURRENT YEAR}} = 13$, and $1+3 = \mathbf{4}$

*This means that on 30 January 2007 you move into a **4** year. On 30 January the following year, this would then move into a **5** year (3+0+1+2+0+0+8 = 14, and 1+4 = **5**), and the year after that, a **6** year, and so on.*

---

2 1 9 8 7 6 5 4 3

Calculation example 2

BIRTHDAY: 21 June 1965

TO CALCULATE THE $2+1+6+\underbrace{2+0+0+7}_{\text{CURRENT YEAR}}=18$, and $1+8 = $ **9**
CURRENT YEAR NUMBER:

This means that on 21 June 2007 you move into a 9 year. On 21 June the following year, this would then move into a 1 year (2+1+6+2+0+0+8 = 19, and 1+9 = 10, and 1+0 = 1), and the year after that, a 2 year, and so on.

Many numerologists feel that the impact of a year number can be felt from the first day of that year – in other words, from 1st January. However, the usual school of thought is that the new number cycle is initiated *on your birthday itself*, and my experience tends to corroborate this. So, if your birthday is fairly late in the year – November or December, say – this means that you will have gone through most of the calendrical year before *your* new

3	4	5	6	7	8	9	1	2

number-year cycle for that year begins.

Look back over some recent years, and see if – in the descriptions on the following pages – you can pinpoint the moment when your yearly number-cycle for any given year became apparent. You'll be amazed at just how accurate this system seems to be.

A 1 year

This is the perfect time to set up new and quite specific long-term goals, and consider just where you want to be a few years from now. You will have new people around you from this point on, and fresh ideas about them and the interests they awaken in you. This is a completely new chapter in your life, and you should set goals for a better and more fulfilling future.

Career-wise, a **1** year often occurs at a time of new employment, or of a complete change in direction in your working life. You are probably wanting to develop new skills or make use of untested talents. You have to believe in yourself now. This is the time when it's a little easier to step back and see how to get started along a particular path. Goals, you will understand, are perfectly attainable, even if a year ago they seemed unrealistic. In a **1** year you have tremendous focus and independence, and excellent determination.

The secret to your success now is in your ability to concentrate; but, emotionally, things can be quite testing. No matter how strong a love bond may be in your life, a **1** year demands that you do much for yourself. You could feel isolated or unsupported, even if someone dear is close by. This is a test of your own courage and inner strength. Only your strongest desires will gain results ... but then, your desires should be fierce during this cycle. Try not to act impulsively, as the push to do so will be powerful, but also, don't be afraid to be independent and go your own way. Strong urges are driving you – forward, for the most part – and a **1** year lends you exceptional clarity and energy.

A 2 year

A year which demands co-operation and partnerships at every level, **2** is a gentle year cycle, when you can consolidate what you started in the previous twelve months. You will need to be diplomatic and sensitive towards other people's feelings, but your intuition is very strong now, and you are able to share the load and the initiative more than you were allowed last year. For this reason, don't try to push things too far or too fast. After the previous whirlwind year, this is a moment to take your time and get things right.

Relationships come more into focus during a **2** year. This is especially pleasing if someone new entered your life in the last year or so, for the vibration of **2** helps a bond to strengthen, and a feeling of mutuality improves now. In some ways you may feel the desire or the need to be secretive, but this is because there are unknown elements at work all on fronts. It will affect you at work and at play, and in a close tie you will discover new tenderness that will probably separate you from other friends. If there is no one special currently in your life, this may be the year to find someone: a **2** year brings a relationship much stronger than a fling!

Your negotiation skills and ability to guess what another person is feeling may work very well for you this year; and, if the number **2** derives from master number **11** (which it almost surely will), there is a chance for serious partnerships and master opportunities. You will need to look at contracts carefully, and spend time on legalities. But this is often the most exciting and unusual year out of the nine. Mysteries come to light, and your ideas flow well. Just be prepared to consider another person in every equation.

A 3 year

Time for you! This twelve-month period is concerned with developing your abilities and testing your flexibility. Your imagination is especially strong, and you may have particular opportunities to improve your wealth and make lasting friendships. You will also need to be focused, because the energy of a **3** year is fast and furious, and may make you feel dissolute. Usually, though, this is a happy year spent with some travel prospects and many creative inspirations. Difficulties which intruded in the previous two years are often resolved in this year cycle.

Business and your social life often run together in a **3** year, and work will be a lot of fun. It is worth taking time over your appearance and indulging yourself more than usual, for the sociability of this number brings you many invitations and a chance to create a new look, or to explore

3   4   5   6   7   8   9   1   2

other aspects of your personality. You have extra charm this year, so try to use it where it is needed.

Many people find that the number **3** expresses itself in a year cycle as a third person to consider: frequently, this is the birth of a child or an addition to the family, but it might be that another party pressures you in your personal relationship. Don't talk too much about this, or show nervousness. Under a **3** vibration, it is easy to become exhausted – even through over-excitement – so be alert to the impulse towards extravagance and fragmentation. Try to enjoy the way in which you are being drawn out of yourself this year, and allow yourself time to study, write, paint. Anything you really want you can achieve now – even strange wishes and desires can be pulled towards you. Make sure you think a little about what you are asking for!

A 4 year

A much-needed year of good-housekeeping – on the personal level, as well as literally. This year will demand practicality from you. Often a **4** brings a focus on money or accounts, on repairs around the home, or on putting your life into better order. It may not be what you want, yet it will force itself upon you. It is sometimes a year spent with a pen in hand – writing lists or cheques, doing sums and keeping diaries. It is also a year when you will need to do some research, to find out about what you don't know.

You have so much work to do in a **4**, or **22**, year – more than for a long time. Your personal pleasure takes second place to requirement, and it may seem difficult to stick to the task sometimes. Money demands that you do so, for extra expenditure is not advised in this twelve-month period. Yet if this sounds stressful, it also gives you a feeling of satisfaction that you will achieve so much this year – a job of hard work and dedication really well done. It may be that this year gives you a very good foundation for the future and sets up lasting improvements.

You will never survive a **4** – or, especially, a **22** – year if you are not organized and implement a system of work and life. Be honest in what you do with others, but also in what you do for yourself. You cannot deceive yourself, and must check details carefully. You may have a feeling of burden at times, but there is a chance to feel you have done something extraordinary too. Translate your clever ideas into practical results. The most significant thing for you to do is to concentrate on proper personal management. The weight of the world is on your shoulders, but you can bear it if the preparations you make are good. There is no escape from demands on your time and intelligence, but nothing can be hurried, so face the job ahead and you will soon find you have climbed a hill to new vistas.

2   1   9   8   7   6   5   4   3

A 5 year

After careful management of your time last year, and a feeling of being tied to the wheel, this will seem like bursting from the inside of a darkened room into bright light. Now you have a change from routine to madness, and you may feel a personal freedom that was denied you last year. Nevertheless, nothing is completely settled in a **5** year, and this uncertainty may take its toll. Try to look at this cycle as a chance to find success in newer areas, and a way to advance from necessary stagnation into running waters of energy and vitality. You will update your sense of yourself during this period, and make progress towards the life you want, following the previous year's required self-discipline.

You are admitting to the need for new pastures, so your ideas of what your life might include, or who may have a role in it, may alter now. No one likes to be held back in a **5** year, but it is still important not to be too hasty in your actions. Use your energies, by all means, but govern them with your head. This is the time for innovation, and new takes on old goals, but if you quarrel with those dear to you, or with whom you work, it may be difficult to repair later. If change is still inevitable, be as kind and constructive as possible, and make sure you aren't leaping from one difficult situation straight into another. You need to discover your versatility and personal resourcefulness to get the best out of this cycle. And, for some of the twelve months, travel or lots of movement seems inescapable.

This year is potentially some kind of turning point for you. Learning how to adapt to sudden circumstances is vital, because any plans or directives set in stone will cause you pain, and possibly come unstuck. Be prepared for changes and, if this brings a nervousness with it, try to meet the adventure head-on. If you talk yourself up and take on a front-running position, you can work wonders in a **5** year.

2   1   9   8   7   6   5   4   3

A 6 year

Love is in the air. Other things seize your time too – your home needs attention, and duties demand your energy – but, principally, this year is about emotions and relationships. Sometimes love and happiness are a reward for surviving so much in the past two years, and for unselfish service and support for others. The emphasis is on finding harmony with others, and this may come in various ways. This year, you may have the impetus and opportunity to erase problems that have previously beset you. You understand, and feel acutely sensitive towards, others, and are more radiant and beautiful than you have been for some time. If you can be kind and positive in emotional dealings, you will benefit in many ways, including materially.

There are hurdles in a **6** year in connection with obligations you feel towards others. At times you are stretched,

3	4	5	6	7	8	9	1	2

because there are personal desires and ties you want to nurture which are countermanded by the duties you are subjected to. You may resent this, yet, if you can remain cheerful, you will be rewarded in ways not immediately apparent. Love is trying to sweep you off your feet, but your health may suffer because you are trying to fit in so much, and the intensity of your feelings is strong.

While it's good to be helpful in a **6** year, don't allow yourself to be taken advantage of, or let people drain you completely. Set up a system that lets you delegate some responsibility. Your home may bloom while you're in such a happy mood, and you should feel creative and mellow. The events of a **6** year are not as fast and furious as the previous year, but things move steadily towards a happier state of being. Let the time go as it will, because this is not a year to fight against what comes to you; get into the right philosophical gear and open yourself to pleasant surprises that come from being useful, and being warm with others.

2   1   9   8   7   6   5   4   3

A 7 year

This year is a time for manifesting your goals by visualizing them. See yourself triumphing and continuing toward your vision. Never lose sight of what you want, or confusion will reign. You'll be tempted this way and that, annoyed by gossip, and attacked by those who love you but don't understand what you are trying to do. Don't be swayed by them, or you will lose your opportunities and precious time.

Keep your head, as everything depends on your state of mind. Refuse to react to distractions, and avoid hasty actions or sudden decisions. A calm approach is the best remedy to the chaos surrounding you. You may have to move house without warning, but take it in your stride and make a calm, clear choice on where to go. If you are travelling somewhere exotic, be prepared with vitamins

3   4   5   6   7   8   9   1   2

and medicines to avoid viruses of any kind.

Legal matters may arise during this year, relating to business, investments or house options. Consult an expert to avoid pitfalls, and, when you feel happy, proceed with confidence. If you have taken all the facts and details into account, you'll now be within sight of your goal. But watch your health, as the number **7** is connected with this subject for both good and ill. You might get fit and lose some weight or, conversely, suffer with some little grievance. This is a time for mental, spiritual and physical detoxing. Also, rest: take a vacation to the country, to a quiet location where you can think in peace. Let no one confuse you. You may have to wait, but you will know how to come out on top if you listen to your intuition.

This is an excellent year for study, research, writing and reading, and clearing out all the unnecessary people or ideas from your past.

An 8 year

This cycle brings the possible finding of a soulmate. If you're single, you could not have a better chance of meeting that special someone than now. **8** years also relate to money, so you may be caught up with an impossible workload and regard the arrival of such a potentially strong love as poor timing – and perhaps this is why it comes to you, because your attention being taken up elsewhere may be the best reason for someone's admiration. The love vibration you experience under karmic year number **8** may point to a future relationship prospect which has a lasting importance.

For those in settled relationships, pregnancy sometimes comes with this number, and it brings a very special link between the child and their parents. Or, you may experience a deep urge to study a subject that comes easily to you, though you have never learned about it before – a

3   4   5   6   7   8   9   1   2

language, perhaps, or an artistic skill you were attracted to but never developed, but which you now pick up well. Even a professional subject that you seem to grasp quickly will seem more important to perfect than ever before. Partly, this is because **8** year cycles concern making more money, and dealing with the deeply felt past. There are huge opportunities for you in an **8** year, and you will want to be prepared to maximize them. However, you'll need to use good judgement and be efficient with your time management.

Many people feel pushed to the limit in an **8** year, because there is just so much going on. Consider, though, that the vibration of the number wants to find positive expression, so the more efficiency and determination you can bring to it, the better the chance of finishing on a high note. Don't over-commit your time or money, and be ready to acquiesce to others' ways of doing things. You need to be confident, but ready to adjust too. **8** is made up of two circles, asking 'infinity' of you. But this year, you can do it!

A 9 year

Your personal affairs all come to a head in a **9** year, and whatever has been insufficient, or unsatisfying, will rise to the surface and demand change now. It could be the fulfilment of many dreams, for this is the culmination of nine years' experience. Whatever is jettisoned was probably no longer of use – though this might seem dispassionate. Many friendships will drift away, but you have probably outgrown them. The strongest demand of you is a readiness to discard what will not be part of your serious future – and this can mean a temporary feeling of insecurity.

You will certainly travel in a **9** year. Even if a trip is short, or of no great distance, it will settle something in your mind. The more compassionate, tolerant and forgiving you are, the more warmth and generosity will come to you. This is not the right moment to start something completely new, but if events arise as a natural conclusion to what has gone before, this is a good thing. Your mind needs to engage with bigger issues, for selfishness or petty ideas will cause you unhappiness under this number. People will thwart you in your career and personal matters – and these obstacles seem to come out of the blue, and are beyond your control. However, if you think on philosophical issues and remain open to big ideas, everything will turn out well.

A **9** year can be populated with many friends and activities, yet can feel lonely too; this is a cycle for completion of tasks and the ending of what is not enduring. But this is the right time to see the fruits of your previous work. Be wise about where your destiny seems to want to take you. Your artistic and imaginative facilities are inspired now, and you'll begin to see new directions that you know you must investigate in the years ahead. You know what is missing in your life, or where you've failed yourself, and can now prepare for the new adventure that's about to dawn.

2 1 9 8 7 6 5 4 3

How to find your DAY NUMBER

Add the digits for the day of birth, and keep adding them until they reduce to one number:

EXAMPLES:

30 January 1971   3+0 = **3**

21 June 1965   2+1 = **3**

How to find your LIFE NUMBER

Add the digits for the day, month and year of birth, and keep adding them until they reduce to one number:

EXAMPLES:

30 January 1971   3+0+1+1+9+7+1 = 22 (a 'master' number), and 2+2 = **4**

21 June 1965   2+1+6+1+9+6+5 = 30 and 3+0 = **3**

Further reading

The Complete Book of Numerology, David A. Phillips, Hay House, 2006

*The Day You Were Born: A Journey to Wholeness Through Astrology and
Numerology*, Linda Joyce, Citadel Press, 2003

Many Things on Numerology, Juno Jordan, De Vorss Books, 1981

Numerology, Hans Decoz and Tom Monte, Perigee Books, 2001

Numerology: The Romance in Your Name, Juno Jordan, De Vorss Books,
1977

Sacred Number, Miranda Lundy, Wooden Books, 2006

*The Secret Science of Numerology: The Hidden Meaning of Numbers
and Letters*, Shirley Blackwell Lawrence, New Page Books, 2001

About the author

Titania Hardie is Britain's favourite 'Good Witch' and a best-selling
author. Born in Sydney, Australia, Titania has a degree in English and
Psychology, and also trained in parapsychology and horary astrology.
With a high media profile, she regularly appears on television in the UK,
US, Canada, Australia and South Africa, as well as receiving widespread
newspaper and magazine coverage. Her previous titles have sold over a
million copies worldwide, and include *Titania's Crystal Ball*, *Aroma Magic*,
and *Hocus Pocus*. Her first novel is due to be published in summer 2007.

Acknowledgements

Many thanks to you, Nick, for the clear and brilliant vision; you knew what you wanted and, like a true and inspired **1**, kept mulling it over until a way was found. This is your baby. Also big thanks to Tessa, master number **22**, for your commitment to this magnum opus beyond call: only you and I know, Tessa, how much time and soul has gone into all of these words. To Ian, for keeping us piping along with a true **4**'s sanguine approach to such a long body of work, and to Elaine and Malcolm for the look – **6**s, naturally! For my daughter Samantha, thanks for some of your ideas which found expression in the second-to-last section: I love the latte in Soho while signing the author. Let's see! To Georgia, for work in the field on number **5**, my thanks. To all of you, my appreciation, and I wish you all LUCKY NUMBERS!

EDDISON·SADD EDITIONS

Editorial Director **Ian Jackson**
Managing Editor **Tessa Monina**
Proofreader **Nikky Twyman**

Art Director **Elaine Partington**
Mac Designer **Malcolm Smythe**
Production **Sarah Rooney**